The Student's Edition
Level I

THE RENAISSANCE PROPHET'S MANUAL

Bishop R. S. Walker

The Student's Edition
Level I

THE
RENAISSANCE PROPHET'S
MANUAL

Bishop Rodney S. Walker I

US Copyright TXu-913-410

US Copyright TXu-243-448

ISBN-13: 978-0692453438

ISBN-10: 0692453431

Printed in the United States of America

Published by Bishop R. S. Walker Ministries formerly
Another Touch of Glory Press
2760 Crain Highway
Waldorf, Maryland 20601
Voice (301-843-9267) - Fax (240-585-7093)
Web address:www.bishoprswalker.com
 E-mail: admin@bishoprswalker.com

Contents

Foreword 6

INTRODUCTION 7

SEASON #1—THE METAMORPHOSIS PROCESS 9

Chapter 1—The Metamorphosis Process 11
    Chapter 1—Chapter Review 14

Chapter 2—Is the Prophetic for Today? 15
    The Program Design 15
    The Mysteries of Christ 16
    Chapter 2—Chapter Review 18

Chapter 3—What Is a Prophet? 19
    Jesus' Ministry 20
    The Mouthpiece of God 21
    Understanding Dispensations 22
    Type of Christ 22
    The Nature of God 23
    The Holy Spirit 24
    Chapter 3—Chapter Review 26

Chapter 4—The Call of the Prophet 27
    Prophetic Maturity 28
    The Samuel Complex 29
    The Jeremiah Complex 30
    The Isaiah Complex 30
    The Jonah Complex 31
    The Habakkuk Complex 32
    Was Your Call Direct or Indirect? 33
    Chapter 4—Chapter Review 36

Chapter 5—The Prophetic and Intercession 37
    Introduction 37
    Keep Mercy and Judgment 37
    Seers vs. Prophets 38
    Understanding Regional Authority 39
    Chapter 5—Chapter Review 41

Chapter 6—What Is an Apostle? 42

The Reestablishing of the Apostolic Office 42

Recognizing Your Call 45

The Marks of a True Apostle 46

Chapter 6—Chapter Review 54

Chapter 7—The Prophets' and Apostles' Call to Personal Balance 55

God-ward Relationship 55

Brother and Sister Relationship 56

Spousal Relationship 57

Chapter 7—Chapter Review 59

SEASON #2—SEASON OF CHALLENGED PURPOSE 61

Chapter 8—Understanding the Father–Son Relationship 63

Father–Son Relationship From an Earthly Perspective 63

Father–Son Relationship From a Heavenly Perspective 67

The Teknon Component 67

The Huios Component 68

The Responsibility Component 68

The Vulnerability Component 70

The Covenant Component 70

The Blessing Component 71

Learning to Father Leaders 71

Leaving Your Comfort Zone and Place of Support, v.12 .72

Shining for or in Another Man's Dream, v.16 73

Preaching Another Man's Word, v.17 73

Locating Your Sons, vv.18-19 74

Leaving the Natural Father and Cleaving to the Spiritual Father, v.20 74

Chapter 8—Chapter Review 75

Chapter 9—The Purpose of the Prophet 76

To Locate Lost Children 76

To Pour Into Sons and Daughters 78

To Declare and Create 79

To Set Order 82

To Prophesy and to Operate in Prophecy 85

To Impart Gifts 86

To Speak to the Hearts of Kings 95

To Establish Churches, Ministries, Businesses, and Training Facilities 97

Chapter 9—Chapter Review 99

Chapter 10—The New Testament Prophet **100**
    To Become a Voice of God 101
    To Receive Prophetic Responsibility 101
    To Illustrate Accountability 102
    To Usher in Change 102
    Chapter 10—Chapter Review 104

Chapter 11—The Development of the Prophet **105**
    The Undeveloped, Underdeveloped and Developed Prophet 105
    The Budding Prophet 109
    Chapter 11—Chapter Review 116

Chapter 12—Who Qualifies for the Prophetic? **117**
    The Beginning Stages 117
    Fine-Tuning the Prophet 117
    Did God Call You? 118
    Can You Handle Being Disliked? 119
    Can You Take Loneliness? 119
    The Test of Being Offended 119
    Handling Intimidation 120
    Can You Take Rejection? 120
    What Type of Prophet Am I? 121
    Prophetic Calling 122
    Serving Until Your Dreams Die 123
    The Attitude of the Prophet 123
    Chapter 12—Chapter Review 126

About the Author **127**
Contact Information **128**

FOREWORD

I think Rodney has touched the heart of God relative to this apostolic and prophetic season that we now embrace. The voice of the Lord is clarion. Not only are we hearing him speak, we are seeing what he's saying. To miss the truth of his message is to be lost.

I'm convinced that as we see the end approach, the prophetic move of the Lord will only escalate. Consequently, we must increase our sensitivity to hear exactly what He is saying, the way He says it, and the context in which He wants us to comprehend His truth. Any deviation from the truth becomes error. Yet, there are many exercising this gift of prophecy with seemingly little or no concern for the exactness of His word or recognition of divine patterns that are prerequisites of certain promised blessings.

For these prophets, every promise seems to be unconditional, as if God is just going to do this, that or the other anyhow. When what has been prophesied fails to come to pass, the poor expectant person becomes utterly disappointed and often cynical about the church and its God.

One way to reduce the "at risk" believers who float from church to church and from one conference to the next seeking "a word" is to bring integrity back to the position of the prophet. The real prophet of the Lord must not be intimated when there's a need to prophesy "woes" as well as blessings. Likewise, the prophet must know the ways of God, so as not to contradict the patterns and prerequisites that are set forth in the scriptures before blessings can flow. Prophets often know the thin line between truth and error. One step in the wrong direction may indeed sound better, but could be the difference between truth and error. To avoid leading those who are hungry for a word into error, we must raise up prophets who see "character" as an absolutely indispensable component. The key is to remember that we do not speak our own thoughts or ideas; we have a God-given responsibility to speak only what the Lord says, the way the Lord says it, in the same context in which He gives it. Lord, help us to raise prophets with character!

As key leaders and mentors in ministry, we must take seriously our responsibility to raise prophets after the heart of God. Prophesying blessings must not become a fad or an occasion to get people hyped. Let's remember that it's knowing the truth that makes us free! Anything else spells bondage and, ultimately, destruction.

Bishop Ralph L. Dennis
Presiding Prelate, Kingdom Fellowship Covenant Ministries
Senior Pastor, Kingdom Worship Center/CFWC
CEO, Ralph L. Dennis Ministries
Towson, Maryland

INTRODUCTION

A renaissance prophet is a person who has experienced a new birth into the call of the office of the prophet and is matured and skilled with the ability to operate in the full capacity of the office of the prophet. He or she has great ability to function in many different areas. This prophet is a cutting-edge prophet who is very knowledgeable in various areas.

The name "renaissance" was selected because it best represents the description of the seasoned matured prophet who has stayed the course long enough to endure every season.

Renaissance is a name given to the "rebirth" of all that was dead and dying in the darkness. During the Renaissance era in world history, there was a rebirth of classical knowledge, the arts, and political and social systems. Renaissance thinking is characterized by a rejection of traditional methods and bringing new life to any given situation. The people who introduced the Renaissance were people who focused on acquiring knowledge through the newly developed ideas naturally and spiritually. Therefore, a renaissance man is considered to be a highly cultivated person who is skilled and well-versed in all areas of arts and sciences. Similarly, the renaissance prophet is well-versed in all areas of the office of the prophet and operates accordingly to bring new life, to revive, to restore, to rebuild, and to reform in an uncommon, non-traditional manner all areas of the human condition. The Renaissance was a time of change for the church and served as the foundation for the Protestant Reformation. God will always send a prophet to introduce change.

This new birth of the renaissance prophet comes at the onset of acknowledgement of the call as a prophet of God. The new fledgling prophet must be developed into a renaissance prophet. This book teaches about the developmental seasons that a prophet must go through and what is required before the prophet reaches the final season of maturity.

The renaissance prophet is a mature prophet who has successfully completed all five of the seasons of development that every prophet must go through to accomplish the assignment of the office of the prophet. This book gives detailed information about the assignment of the office of the prophet and the seasonal changes that mature the renaissance prophet. Once prophets reach the maturity season of their prophetic lives, they operate with the Holy Spirit to accomplish every good work assigned to their hands.

God will allow a renaissance prophet to speak to a person or situation without having first spoken about the subject Himself. God can trust a renaissance prophet to speak for Him, and He releases the prophet to operate according to His plan and purpose.

The renaissance prophet has authority to invoke revival, introduce and implement life-changing innovations, remove waste and unneeded activity, bring about increase and multiply provision in the natural and in the spiritual realm, pioneer changes prophetically, and speak for God as His mouthpiece in any environment, in any culture, or under any circumstances.

God has great expectations of renaissance prophets. They are expected to make an exchange or bring change while operating according to the Word of God and the will of God, exercise the authority given them as fully matured prophets, and be knowledgeable (having a full understanding of all areas of the assignment and the office of the prophet), skilled, and seasoned, knowing what, when, and how to do what needs to be done with the help of the Holy Spirit in any given prophetic situation.

When people are seeking God for answers, the renaissance prophet always has an answer from God. The prophet is able to speak life into dead situations; change darkness to light; stop devastation of storms caused by the Devil in the natural and in the spiritual realms; bring in new ideas, processes, and procedures in areas where that particular item has never been done before; pioneer new inventions; introduce innovation that will change the course of direction and places; and stop the killing cycle (when the Devil is killing a large group of people, dreams, or ideas).

The process of becoming is the beginning of the life cycle of a renaissance prophet; it is a comprehensive and complete process of development. As you read this book, it is my prayer that you submit to the whole development process to become that renaissance prophet, "Being confident of this very thing, that he which hath begun a good work in you will perform it until the day of Jesus Christ." (Phil. 1:6)

SEASON #1
THE METAMORPHOSIS
PROCESS

meta[mor[pho[sis

n., pl. **-[ses** (-sez) < Gr *metamorphosis* < *metamorphoun,* to transform, transfigure < *meta,* over (see META-) + *morphe,* form, shape]

1 *a*) change of form, shape, structure, or substance; transformation, the form resulting from such change

2 a marked or complete change of character, appearance, condition, etc.

3 *Biol.* a change in form, structure, or function as a result of development; specif., the physical transformation, more or less sudden, undergone by various animals during development after the embryonic state, as of the larva of an insect to the pupa and the pupa to the adult, or of the tadpole to the frog

4 *Med.* a pathological change of form of some tissues

(taken from *Webster's New World Dictionary*)

CHAPTER 1—The Metamorphosis Process

Metamorphosis: 1. A change of physical form, structure, or substance especially by supernatural means. 2. A striking alteration in appearance, character, or circumstances. 3. A marked and more or less abrupt developmental change in the form or structure of an animal (as a butterfly or a frog) occurring subsequent to birth or hatching.
—taken from *Webster's Collegiate Dictionary*

It's time for the change…

Imagine, all of this time you have existed as no one but yourself. You have been whatever your name happens to be. Now that you know Jesus, you are still the same person you were, but you have Jesus in your life. You've become conscious of who you are to be in Him; but massive changes have not yet taken place because you have not yet entered ministry.

Because you have not entered ministry at this point, your proverbial boat remains calm and steady. There is no shaking. In fact, your boat has never really been shaken before. In contrast, the minute you accept ministry, your boat begins to shake and rock. It is at this very moment that you begin to become someone you've never known before.

Jesus hand-picked some people whom He absolutely shook! In essence, He disturbed the foundations of who they were. Those who had been chosen figured that they were simply acknowledging a call. Well, what happens when you acknowledge a call?

Remember, you said that you would go, you said that you would do this and that. These declarations initiated the process of metamorphosis. The course of change has now found you. The person you've known all of this time now begins to become obsolete and foreign to you. You must learn that you can no longer make decisions based who you have been, but according to the person whom you are becoming, even though you don't know *what* you are becoming.

The process of metamorphosis may best be seen in the life of the tadpole. Tadpoles were born in the creek. These little guys have lived the simple life. They just swim around the creek to their hearts' content. They grow and grow and become bigger and bigger, but they still have that tail and continue to swim around their precious little creek. If you watch tadpoles long enough, however, you'll find that they will begin to grow legs. But even with these newly formed legs, they're still swimming!

The problem is that the tadpoles are actually becoming what they have never been before. Eventually all of the tadpoles will develop into frogs. Tadpoles don't look like frogs at all. But change sets in. The tadpoles start to take on another physical form or structure. Not only will their form change, but their operation will change as well.

A tadpole, at the set time and the set moment, will lose its tail and mature from wagging its tail to leaping. It will leap farther than anything else in the water can leap. Nonetheless, this is not the limit of the tadpole's transformation. As a tadpole, it was confined to the boundaries of water. As a frog, the tadpole becomes amphibious.

The frog is an amazing creature. The frog is not confined to the water. It can go underwater and emerge onto dry land at its leisure. But let us not forget, it didn't start out as a frog; its life began as a tadpole. The process of metamorphosis took place, and the tadpole became something it had never been before. The frog began to do things it had never done before. The frog became something it had never known before.

Likewise, the caterpillar that had only been accustomed to crawling around on the ground also met change. It had only been a caterpillar that had also been confined to a particular area. It had never known the experience of flying, and at the set time and at the set moment, it became able to fly. How does this really happen? Why? The answer: metamorphosis.

You and I are like tadpoles and caterpillars. We are becoming what we've never been before, and we don't understand it. We don't understand what's happening in us. Yet, we are still becoming.

It is the will of God that we become what He desires that we become. Why do you think that some of us fail to become? Has a tadpole, which was born a tadpole, ever set its will to not become a frog? Has a caterpillar, which was born a caterpillar, ever set its will to not become a butterfly? Absolutely not! Neither of these creatures had a choice in their metamorphosis process. We, on the other hand, do have a choice.

We are the only ones that were created in the image and the likeness of God. No other creature on the planet has been so privileged. We have been given a will that we can set to submit to the plan of God or to fight against the plan of God.

We make the decision, as prophets, prophetic people, and men and women of God to become. Sure, the road to becoming is very painful. Conversely, the road to resistance is even more painful. The road to becoming is laden with benefits. The road to resistance is laden with penalties. Pain is inevitable, but the pain that you prefer is your decision alone. Make the right choice.

The choice to become is left totally in your hands. The process of metamorphosis is designed to develop you into what is in the mind of God. If you yield to the process, the pain will prove to be worthwhile, and becoming what God has destined you to be will be unavoidable. If you resist the process, the pain will prove to be unbearable and unnecessary, and what God has destined you to be will follow you to your grave.

13

CHAPTER 1—Chapter Review

1. Define metamorphosis within the context of the lesson.

2. Identify some of the ways that you are cooperating with the process of becoming. What tangible benefits do you see?

3. Identify some of the ways that you are not cooperating with the process of becoming. Based on the information provided in this chapter, what would you do differently?

CHAPTER 2—Is the Prophetic for Today?

"…Upon this rock I will build my church…" (Matt. 16:18) was Jesus' prophetic proclamation of the New Testament. Jesus preached, taught, and demonstrated the power of the gospel of the kingdom of God as portrayed by Matthew. He presented the spiritual and heavenly kingdom that could be entered into only by repentance and faith. The kingdom of God was given to a nation that would bring forth the fruits thereof; thus the background was set for the building of His church.

Ephesians 4 depicts the gifts given by Jesus that establish the structure of church leadership. Ephesians 4 gives an exhortation of the privileges and responsibilities of the Christian through unity and love. It also includes an explanation of how "the body" (of the church) would be led and the means by which it would function and mature. The "ascension gifts" (ministry) are commonly referred to as the "five-fold ministry." The foundational purposes for these gifts are also described in Ephesians 4:12-13.

The apostle Paul prophetically reveals in Ephesians 4 that everything the body of Christ would need to grow and mature was established by Jesus, as seen in verse eight: *"…When he ascended up on high, he led captivity captive, and gave gifts unto men."* As we examine specifically the gift of the prophet, we will identify the prophet's purpose.

The "ascension gifts" brought authority, order, and structure to the church. The apostle Paul further depicts the ranking responsibility in the order of the apostle, prophet, evangelist, pastor, and teacher.

> **And he gave some, apostles; and some, prophets; and some, evangelists; and some, pastors and teachers… Ephesians 4:11**

The Program Design

This program is designed to identify and bring clarity of understanding to the ranking authority, positions, roles, and responsibilities of the prophetic ministry and how the prophet contributes to:

1. The perfecting of the saints,
2. The work of the ministry, and
3. The edification (building up) of the "body of Christ."

The Word of God also shows us the duration that these gifts will be with us:

1. Till we all come into the unity of the faith,
2. And of the knowledge of the Son of God;
3. Unto a perfect man;
4. Unto the measure of the stature of the fullness of Christ.

In today's church, the prophets **have not** fulfilled their role and purpose. Without the prophets active in their role in today's church, the church has become less effective than she would have been if the order and plan of God for the church had been followed through.

The role of the prophet is essential to bringing certain aspects of God's Word and order to the body of Christ. **They must show the way, even in their times of testing.**

Among the reasons for the prophets are:

1. So that we do not continue to be children tossed to and fro.
2. So that we are not carried about with every wind of doctrine (teaching) as Ephesians 4:15 says:

> **But speaking the truth in love, may grow up into him in all things, which is the head, even Christ: Ephesians 4:15**

The Mysteries of Christ

This is what is called the "Mysteries of Christ." Why? As we carry out the work of His ministry, we are (mysteriously or secretly) hidden in Him. Jesus' great end and design in giving gifts unto men was intended for the well-being of His church.

All of the ascension gifts were given for a certain period of time. That period of time is identified by the word "UNTIL" (which indicates continuance); the church has not yet come in

16

unity and maturity. Therefore, the church is still in need of the ascension gift ministry.

Key Point: *"Until" the church comes into unity and maturity, there will always be the need for the ascension gifts.*

The body is divided because of denominations. This is one reason why only part of the fulfillment has come to pass.

> **But ye are a chosen generation, a royal priesthood, a holy nation... 1 Peter 2:9**

The Word specifically says that you are to *"give diligence to make your calling and election sure: for if ye do these things, ye shall never fall…* (2 Peter 1:10)

With all of our getting, we must get an understanding. Our next chapter will give us an understanding of what a prophet is.

NOTES

CHAPTER 2—Chapter Review

1. According to Ephesians 4, what are the ascension gifts?

2. What are the functional purposes and program design of these gifts?

3. How would you explain to someone, using scriptural references, that the prophet is still for today and why the prophet is still needed?

CHAPTER 3—What Is a Prophet?

The prophet is a person whom God has chosen for the purpose of revealing His mind to the body of Christ, or the church. Before they were called prophets, they were called "seers" and had the same functions as the Old Testament prophets.

(Beforetime in Israel, when a man went to inquire of God, thus he spake, Come, let us go to the seer: for he that is now called a Prophet was beforetime called a Seer.) 1 Samuel 9:9

There are three terms that are specifically important for designating prophets.

First term: The most important term is the Hebrew word "Nabi." Nabi means to declare or announce. The primary function of the prophet was to declare or announce, or to be one who utters a communication. In the form of a noun, it is used nearly three hundred times in the Old Testament. The other two terms are used much less.

Second term: The Hebrew words "ro'eh" and "hozeh" both mean "one who sees." They are both translated "seer." Hazon is the word that is consistently used for the prophetic vision and is found in Samuel, Chronicles, Psalms, and Proverbs and in most of the books of the prophets.

Third term: Sometimes the prophets are called "watchmen": ("sopin" in Hebrew) in Jeremiah 6:17, and Ezekiel 3:17; 33:2, 6-7 and "shomer," a watchman, in Isaiah 21:11 and 62:6.

We should also mention a fourth term, although it is used less than any other. It is the phrase "man of God" or "Ish-elohim." This term is significant and rare, and simply means or refers to the prophet as one who has been chosen and sent by God.

In the Greek, the word "prophetes" signifies "one who speaks for another," especially "one who speaks for a god" and so inter-

NOTES

prets his will to man. Hence, its essential meaning is "an interpreter."

The English language "prophecy" is the sense of prediction and in this sense has been retained as its popular meaning. The larger sense or use as interpretation has not been lost.

The prophet is called to be the "mouthpiece," or one who speaks on behalf of God. As such, we **must** purpose in ourselves to quickly understand the gravity of who we are and what our role is, and that there will continually be many challenges to this position, both naturally and spiritually.

> **He said unto him, I am a prophet also as thou art; and an angel spake unto me by the word of the Lord, saying, Bring him back with thee into thine house, that he may eat bread and drink water. But he lied unto him. 1 Kings 13:18**

The prophet **must** also understand the reality that his enemy, Satan, will produce other voices in an attempt to enter in and distort the voice of God. Voices that are not of God will lead into false prophecy.

<u>**Key Point**</u>: *Understand that Satan's job is to distort the voice of God.*

Jesus' Ministry

During the period when Jesus walked the earth and throughout the remainder of the New Testament, God never said to anyone, "Go and kill." Killing is not in the plan of God any longer. The reason for this is that after the Old Testament, God's work in the earth was complete, and the door of the earth was open for the introduction of Jesus' ministry to begin, as presented in the four gospels of the New Testament.

Jesus now sits at the right hand of the Father. In Acts 2 and through a portion of the Book of Revelation, the Holy Spirit stood up. The Holy Spirit is standing in His role and responsibility to guide and teach today.

The Mouthpiece of God

The deceiver, Satan, desires to distort the real voice of God. Since the prophet is God's mouthpiece, Satan wants to deceive him and cause him to be in error. Give the Word, but only say what God is saying, not what He seems to be saying.

<u>Key Point</u>: *When we understand and accept that prophets are the "mouthpiece" of God, we will clearly understand the reason Satan attempts to cause us to hear others' voices.*

If the mouthpiece has been proved, tried, and tested, and is fine-tuned in hearing accurately from God, there will be no opportunity for deception in prophesying God's Word. The prophet is responsible for the nation he is in. We will learn that the prophet is also responsible for turning the direction of the town, city, country, nation, and church to which he has been assigned. The prophet is one who must interpret what God is saying to the location (the town, city, country, nation, and church) wherein God has placed him.

Consider what God thinks of His Word. **Remember**, He said that He would exalt His Word above His name. As you think about that, do you realize how important it is to be proven, tried, and tested as a prophet?

The prophet, as well as the apostle, is one who is made "*a spectacle*" (1 Cor. 4:9). The prophet is one who walks alone. If you cannot deal with loneliness, then you do not want to be a prophet. The prophet is one of the most disliked persons that exist. If you cannot deal with being disliked, you must consider whether you are truly called to be a prophet. The Word says that we are fools for Christ. If a person is not willing to look like a fool, he is not ready to be a prophet.

<u>Key Point:</u> *If you are truly called to be a prophet, then stay in training, pray, and come into the reality of your role. If God said you're strong enough, THEN YOU ARE. DO NOT PLAY WITH YOUR CALLING. Many people duck in and out of their call according to what they feel. The Bible says in 1 Corinthians 15:58 (AB), "Therefore, my beloved brethren, be firm (steadfast), immovable, always abounding in the work of the Lord [always being superior, excelling, doing more than enough in the serv-*

NOTES

21

ice of the Lord], knowing and being continually aware that your labor in the Lord is not futile [it is never wasted or to no purpose]."

Understanding Dispensations

Let us understand the dispensations and who was working in each one. A dispensation is an era of time during which man is tested in respect to obedience to some definite revelation of God's will.

1. Genesis to Malachi

From Genesis to Malachi, ultimately it was God doing what needed to be done.

> **In the beginning God created the heaven and the earth. Genesis 1:1**

God speaks or prophesies everything into existence.

> **And God said, Let there be... Genesis 1:3**

God Himself prophesied regarding the hatred between the seed of the serpent and the seed of the woman.

> **And I will put enmity between thee and the woman, and between thy seed and her seed; it shall bruise thy head, and thou shalt bruise his heel. Genesis 3:15**

> **And God said unto Noah, The end of all flesh is come before me; for the earth is filled with violence through them; and behold, I will destroy them with the earth. Genesis 6:13**

Type of Christ

In the Old Testament, we find two significant things that God did until a type of Christ would come on the earth. That type of Christ was the prophet Moses. In Numbers 14:11-16, we read the account of the dialogue between God and Moses regarding Israel's rebellion against God.

God would have destroyed the Israelites and begun a new nation through Moses. But Moses interceded on behalf of the children of Israel, saying to God, "You cannot do that, lest the enemy accuse you of not being able to bring the people out." The first thing that God did was destroy. Second, He created and began a process of replenishing in the earth.

The Nature of God

The second significant act was shown in the nature of God. We see in the Old Testament that God's nature was not only to **create** but also to **destroy**. This act was carried out in **Genesis 6:7** and **Genesis 7:23.** The nature of our holy God's love could not be compromised by the acceptance of mankind's sin.

As we observe the Old Testament prophets, we see that they moved in levels or degrees of prophecy. The anointing would come upon them as God chose to use them. These men and women were wholly separated unto God. He would choose and raise them as His prophets to reveal His mind to the people, the leaders, or nation.

<u>**Key Point**</u>: *The ministry of the Old Testament prophets was always to show the true spiritual meaning behind the strict letter of the law.*

The office of the Old Testament prophets was considered to be somewhat higher than that of the New Testament prophets. There were many similarities between their titles and functions. All Old Testament prophets were forerunners pointing to the pattern prophet—Jesus Christ.

2. The Gospels

The Gospels are the introduction to the "Redeemer" Jesus Christ. The Word said that Jesus came to seek and save the lost, **not to destroy them** (Luke 19:10). It must be clearly understood that the purpose and nature from which Jesus was operating was to bring into the earth salvation for a lost and dying world. The word "salvation" comes from a Greek word that means "deliverance." Throughout the period Christ moved upon the earth, He was deliberately focused on His mission and goals: first, **to re-**

NOTES

deem; second, **to deliver**; third, **to reveal the grace of God**; and fourth, **to establish His church**.

We have entered in under a new covenant because of our Redeemer, Jesus. Jesus made a way for us when situations seemed hopeless. *"…old things are past away; behold all things are become new"* (2 Cor. 5:17). It is because of the new covenant that we now embrace the New Testament. The New Testament prophet came along with that new covenant.

The Holy Spirit

The Holy Spirit came (1) **to sustain** us and stop us from continual falling, and (2) **to enable us** to do that which we possibly could not do prior. The Holy Spirit was purposed to bring forth the fullness of all God intended and to bring balance. Remember, in Matthew 28:19, the other side of the revelation is that the fullness of the Godhead is demanded to be shown … *"baptizing them in the name of the Father and of the Son, and of the Holy Ghost."* The very next verse says, *"teaching them."* Let's talk about that word "baptize." The word "baptize" comes from a Greek word that means to immerse or to dip, to take totally under. Therefore, if the Word says to baptize them in the name of the Father, we must take them totally under in whom the Father is. Who is He? He is both creator and destroyer. God never stepped outside of His purpose and nature. That is why the earth was without form and void, and darkness was upon the face of the deep. For the same reason, Noah was told to build an ark because the destroyer had to do His work and recreate. This time God would start over with Noah. He started over with Adam. What did Adam and Noah have in common? They both were told to replenish the earth.

However, the job of the Holy Spirit is to guide us in all things. John 16:13 says that the Holy Spirit will give the prophet the needed balance in order to enter the fullness of what is inside of us. Colossians 2:9 says, *"For in him dwelleth all the fullness of the Godhead bodily."* Verse ten says, *"and ye are complete in him…"* The Bible further says that we are in Him and He is in us. Therefore, the fullness of the Father, Son, and Holy Spirit is in us. The Holy Spirit sustains us within the boundaries, and He balances us. We have the ability to create and destroy, to redeem through the ministry of reconciliation, and to sustain through love, grace, and mercy. The fullness is in us. Yet, the Holy Spirit teaches us what to do and when to do it as prophets.

A dispensation is an era of time during which man is tested in respect to obedience to some definite revelation of God's will. The period of time that began with the death and resurrection of Christ is known as the "Dispensation of Grace." This period of testing was no longer directed toward legal obedience to the law as a condition of salvation, but toward acceptance or rejection of Christ. As we look at the period of time covered in the New Testament, we understand this is when the Holy Spirit was sent to the earth. The Holy Spirit was and is responsible for preserving that which the Lord has redeemed and saved.

Key Point: *We MUST understand that the Holy Spirit has the awesome responsibility of stabilizing mankind to bring us to a place where we will stop our continual falling.*

Therefore, the Holy Spirit could be recognized as our "enabler." Through the Holy Spirit, the Lord also gave gifts to the body of Christ that would mature them in the things of God. This brings us to the purpose of the New Testament prophets.

NOTES

CHAPTER 3—Chapter Review

1. What is a prophet? Provide scriptural references other than the ones provided in the chapter to support your answer.

2. Why is it important for us to understand who we are as prophets and prophetic people and what our roles are?

3. Why is it important to submit to a process of being proven, tried, and tested? Provide scriptural examples to support your answer.

4. What is a dispensation?

5. Discuss and define the nature of God, Jesus, and the Holy Spirit.

CHAPTER 4—The Call of the Prophet

It is our desire to reveal, through the Word of God, an understanding of some of the many things that are going on within you that have caused you to believe that you have a prophetic calling on your life. There is a tremendous amount of information to be understood about the prophets of God. It is not complicated to understand if this calling is for you.

The Word of God tells us that, *"wisdom is the principle thing…and with all thy getting get understanding."* We desire to impart understanding to you regarding the "call of the prophet."

> **And the Lord said unto Moses, See, I have made thee a god to Pharaoh: and Aaron thy brother shall be thy prophet. Exodus 7:1**

What Aaron was to Moses, we are to Christ in this world. God has chosen or called each of us for a particular role and responsibility in Him. He did this before the foundation of the world. In the case of Moses and Aaron, God instructed Moses and called Aaron to speak to the people and Pharaoh on His behalf.

Throughout the Old Testament, God chose men or women to speak to an individual, the church, and the nation on His behalf.

> **And he said, Hear now my words: If there be a prophet among you, I the Lord will make myself known unto him in a vision, and will speak unto him in a dream. Numbers 12:6**

God established and utilized the role of the prophet in the Old Testament. The order and structure of leadership in the New Testament church was put in place at Jesus' ascension.

> **And he gave some, apostles; and some, prophets; and some, evangelists; and some, pastors and teachers; Ephesians 4:11**

<u>Understand</u>: *Your ministry gifts are never for you. They are never for your gain, but for the perfecting of the saints, the work of the ministry, and the edifying of the body of Christ.*

NOTES

27

As we come to understand the ministry and role of the prophet, we come to realize that his gift is not for himself. Now we must understand the process that it takes to "answer the call."

Those who are "called" must understand that before they ever came into being, God knew and called them. An example of this is found when God told Jeremiah, *"Before I formed thee in the belly, I knew thee…"*

> **Before I formed thee in the belly I knew thee;**
> **and before thou camest forth out of the womb**
> **I sanctified thee, and I ordained thee a prophet**
> **unto the nations. Jeremiah 1:5**

There is nothing that you can do that will catch God by surprise. He knew you before you were anything. God also came into a knowing of what you would do, what you would not do, and every mistake that you would make, yet He still called you and sanctified you.

<u>Understand</u>: *God set you apart for His purpose and for His glory before you came into the world.*

The reason the prophet must and will undergo challenges is so that he or she will experience and understand what it means to be "set apart." For some, the prophetic gifts have been in operation within them since they were children. Don't get the operation of a gift confused with the release of a call or office. Some problems and challenges come because no one was available to fine-tune the prophet in his gift. The proper awareness and training for his or her call would cause the prophet to develop and to answer the call of God. It is necessary for each prophet to go through the period or season when he or she will come to accept Jesus, go through the fire, the desert, and testing; and seek the face of God for himself or herself.

After seeking the face of God and discovering your prophetic calling, there is yet another step: "**prophetic maturity.**"

Prophetic Maturity

The prophet must come into prophetic maturity. Things that were allowed or accepted when they were babies are no longer acceptable. God does not permit excuses. The Lord will no longer allow those in the prophetic to make excuses for why he or she cannot go or cannot obey Him.

As you, a prophet, mature in the prophetic gifts, God does less and less in order to bring you to the place of having face-to-face relationship with Him. God will let you go through the maximum challenges or desert experiences in order that you might come to know His heart. It is time to come to know the heart of God and to move on from just knowing His voice. If you learn the heart of God, you will come to understand what Moses understood. Moses wanted to know of God's way, *"...shew me now thy way...."(Ex. 33:13)*

We want to help you to take the proper steps into maturity that will lead to your ultimate destiny. Therefore, from point to point in your walk, you are setting stones in place in order to fulfill your destiny. We also understand why, at this particular point of our destiny, challenges have prevented us from entering the next phase of our destiny.

All prophetically gifted people deal with some form of complex within them. The majority of the time, the obstacle has much to do with our self-worth. The thought of being unworthy to function in basic prophetic, prophetic gifting, prophetic ministry, or the office of the prophet causes us to make excuse about why we cannot wear the prophetic mantle.

One of the greatest battles that you will ever fight and endure will be the battle of your mind. If the Devil were to ever defeat you and disqualify you in the prophetic, he would have to win the battle of your mind. Therefore, let us guard our minds with everything that we have (Eph. 6:11-18).

Let's look at some Old Testament examples of great prophets who dealt with forms of personal complexes illustrating the mind's battle of unworthiness.

1. The Samuel Complex

Samuel had a problem accepting the call because of his age. He was approximately ten years old when God spoke to him concerning the priest Eli. God would not accept his age as an excuse or as a reason that he shouldn't give Eli the message from God.

NOTES

29

2. The Jeremiah Complex

Jeremiah had a problem accepting his calling because of his age and because of the value he placed on being accepted by people. God would not accept Jeremiah's youth as an excuse for not answering the call. But, God encouraged him. He told Jeremiah in Jeremiah 1:7, *"Say not I am a child…"* and in Jeremiah 1:8, *"Be not afraid of their faces…"* In all of this, God is showing that there will be a time of preparation. There will, no doubt, come **testing and situations in the life of the budding prophet.**

<u>Note</u>: *God wants us to clearly understand that He is always with us to deliver us in any and all circumstances. This confidence helps us to carry out His command to anyone within the ascension gift ministry of the prophetic.*

<u>Understanding</u>: *When Jeremiah said that he could not speak for he was a child, God told him what not to say, and then touched his mouth (Jer. 1:4-10).*

In the life of a prophet, God will always touch that which is incorrect. It's up to the prophet to accept or to reject the touching of God. This is why our study is so very important. If we accept the touching of God, God will perfect us in the areas where we are mentally, spiritually, or physically handicapped.

3. The Isaiah Complex

Isaiah lived among unclean people, and he had an unclean mouth just as the people had. We have to be very mindful that we don't become like the people whom we are helping. Our assignment is to bring change. Amazingly, God did the same for both Isaiah and Jeremiah. He touched their mouths.

> **Then I said, Woe is me! for I am undone; because I am a man of unclean lips, and I dwell in the midst of a people of unclean lips: for mine eyes have seen the King, the Lord of hosts. Isaiah 6:5**

Isaiah declared that, saying he could not speak because he had unclean lips, and he dwelt in the midst of people with unclean lips. Therefore, God touched his mouth, because of his uncleanness, with hot coals. Regardless of how God has to touch one who is to be His mouthpiece, He will touch him or her with a hot coal or with a warm hand. Everyone must have a touch from God (Isa. 6:5-8).

Yet, there was a prophet whose mouth God would not touch. That prophet was Jonah. It is important that we understand how we are being used by God. Is God just using us, or is God pleased to use us? The choice is yours! Let's look at how He used Jonah.

4. The Jonah Complex

Jonah was a man who was concerned about how people would view him. He carried bitterness and resentment against the people of Nineveh, and he was self-exalting. In other words, Jonah had a heart condition that was toward himself and not toward the people. It is important that everyone who has a call to the prophetic office, prophetic ministry, prophetic gifting, or basic prophetic have a heart toward the people and God. We must examine Jonah's life, lest any of us come to the same destiny that Jonah came to. Not only did the Book of Jonah seem not to have a complete end, Jonah was never mentioned any more in terms of a prophetic assignment. Therefore, God used him, but was not pleased to use him.

<u>Understand</u>: *Do not get caught up in <u>desiring</u> that what you speak prophetically to come to pass, <u>especially</u> when it involves condemnation, damnation, and the degradation of the very people whom God wants to bless. Our assignment is to say what God is saying and not to force our manifestation. There were things that Isaiah prophesied that he never saw in his time.*

<u>Key Point</u>: *God wants to bless and save all people. He loves the people, but He hates the sin. We must learn to separate the sin from the person whom we may correctly judge. When the men brought the woman who was taken in adultery, Jesus refused to judge the woman, not being a witness. But He did judge the men who were the carriers of the complaint or sin. They carried the thing that should have been judged. Jesus gave them the opportunity to make a judgment on the woman if they were without sin (John 8:7). Remember to judge the thing or sin and not the person. Let's make the separation. "But he that is spiritual*

31

judgeth all things, yet he himself is judged of no man" (1 Cor. 2:15). Our frame of thought here must be new covenant-minded. Jesus said, "For the Son of man is come to seek and to save that which was lost." (Luke 19:10)

Therefore, prophetic people need to perform a heart examination on themselves in order to bring forth, from within, the very heart of God—that we love the people as He loves the people. The lesson learned from Jonah was that God's grace went beyond the boundaries of Israel to embrace all nations.

5. The Habakkuk Complex

Habakkuk's letter seemed to be filled with complaints about God's not hearing. Habakkuk complained that God would show him situations that He was not willing to change. After his first complaint, God said…

> **Behold ye among the heathen, and regard, and wonder marvelously: for I will work a work in your days, which ye will not believe, though it be told you. Habakkuk 1:5**

I MUST EMPHASIZE: Within the above statement, God is **making a clear statement to prophets!** God is not talking to the people; He is talking to the prophet. He is telling the prophet what He is going to do. A prophet or prophetic people who have the **Habakkuk Complex** will not believe the Word of God told to them. This was because of the break in the pattern to which the prophet was accustomed.

Therefore, it is imperative that we do not get so locked into custom that when God moves in an unorthodox way, we are not able to follow Him.

Key Point: _If you have this kind of problem, you will be limited in what God can say to you._

It is important that your will lines up with God's will, and God's will is in line with His Word. Carnality can interfere with clearly knowing God's will for your life. You do not want to operate in a position to which you were not called. Therefore, you need to know whether your calling as a prophet is direct or indirect.

Was Your Call Direct or Indirect?

In many cases, not all, we walk in areas of ministry for which we have never been called. This is because of the misconception of what we think we have heard. When Samuel heard God call his name, he was not sure who called him. It is normal to hear and not understand what you hear.

Remember: *Most of your prophetic gifting has to do with hearing and speaking.*

Therefore, your first challenge is to hear God regarding your call. You will wrestle with hearing until you hear accurately. The question remains: **Was your call direct or indirect?**

A biblical example of a prophet with an indirect call was Isaiah. It did not take away from the authenticity of his call as a prophet.

Example: *I call a secretary whom I know to do a job, and then someone in my company volunteers for the job. They both are equally secretaries.*

God will grant us the privilege of working for Him in whatever area we desire if He sees that we can pay the price for that area of work. There is a price to pay for every level of the prophetic. I am not sure that God had predetermined that James and John would be a part of the inner cabinet of Jesus. But since they volunteered for the job and were willing to pay the price, Jesus invited them to drink of His cup and to be baptized with His baptism.

Warning: *Do not ask for anything you cannot pay the price for.*

There are people whom God has specifically called into the office of the prophet. He expects them to develop, grow, and blossom where they have been planted. When God plants you in a specific place or office, know that you can blossom there because God planted you there, as difficult as it may seem. Within the prophetic ministry, there is a specific climate that is necessary for your development. God has planted you in a specific climate for a specific reason.

NOTES

A climate is a region or area with certain prevailing weather conditions that affect life, activity, growth, etc. Your climate always has to do with your spiritual season. If you adjust your spiritual thermostat, you are able to control your physical temperature. Yet, adjusting your physical temperature will never change your spiritual thermostat. You can change from church to church, and your season will not change, providing that the difficulties that you are experiencing are actually caused by your season.

1. Indirect Calls

- Isaiah 6:8, "*Also I heard the voice of the Lord, saying, Whom shall I send, and who will go for us? Then I said, Here am I; send me.*"

- Hosea 1:1, "*The word of the Lord that came unto Hosea, the son of Beeri, in the days of Uzziah, Jotham, Ahaz, and Hezekiah, kings of Judah.*"

- Malachi 1:1, "*The burden of the word of the Lord to Israel by Malachi.*" It is uncertain whether Malachi was called directly or indirectly. If Malachi was in fact his name, we are led to believe that he was directly called. The name Malachi means "my messenger" or "Jehovah's messenger."

2. Direct Calls

- Exodus 3:4, "*And when the Lord saw that he turned aside to see, God called unto him out of the midst of the bush, and said Moses, Moses. And he said, Here am I.*"

- 1 Samuel 3:10, "*And the Lord came, and stood, and called as at other times, Samuel, Samuel. Then Samuel answered, Speak; for thy servant heareth.*"

- Jeremiah 1:5, "*Before I formed thee in the belly I knew thee; and before thou camest forth out of the womb I sanctified thee, and I ordained thee a prophet unto the nations.*"

Stay tuned to the voice of God. Many distractions will come. It is important that you stay focused and walk in your calling. Why is that important? It is important because you have a preordained destiny. You're going for the goal; you must be able to recognize **"the touching of God."**

CHAPTER 4—Chapter Review

1. Why does the prophet undergo challenges?

2. Is operation of a gift the same as being released in the call or office? Please explain and support your answer with scriptural references.

3. Describe prophetic maturity.

4. Describe the five complexes discussed in this chapter and the areas God had to touch in order to bring about perfection.

CHAPTER 5—The Prophetic and Intercession (Hosea 12:6)

Introduction

As we look at the setting in Hosea 12:1-6, we find both the nation of Judah and the nation of Israel in a backslidden condition and God calling the people back to repentance and fellowship with Him. As an example, we can use Jacob, who struggled with God to make it back to a place of favor in Him. It is important to see whom God called to this place of intercession for the people. God calls for the prophet as a seer to intercede for the people and to prophesy the people into destiny. Before doing so, the seer/intercessor comes to break up fallow ground. The seer/intercessor will come to melt the hearts of the hardhearted and to clear the atmosphere of hindrances. This kind of Word is easily received once the seer/intercessor has done this job. God is saying, "Return!"

Keep Mercy and Judgment

Mercy is the place of meditation, a place of intercession, and where we prefer others above ourselves. Although people who are in the office of the prophet are not mercy-driven, God powerfully moves through them in prophetic intercession as the mind and purpose of God are revealed to them. While interceding and being sensitized to what God desires to happen, they are under strict orders not to speak but to pray as intercessors.

> **Let us therefore come boldly unto the throne of grace, that we may obtain mercy, and find grace to help in time of need. Hebrews 4:16**

So here we come into intercession with a real sense of dying to who we are, and to whom we think we are, as we become aware of our place of intercession. In the counseling session, you don't look to say much for yourself.

Look at this as **inter-session**. You enter a session to make something happen for someone else.

NOTES

Seers vs. Prophets

Through and by this spirit of prophecy, God desires to use the church to bring change in the life of the world. This is where the anointing to prophesy will come on a spirit-filled vessel. The important issue is that we remember that this is still not the seer/intercessor.

> **And the Lord came down in a cloud, and spake unto him, and took of the spirit that was upon him, and gave it unto the seventy elders: and it came to pass, that when the spirit rested upon them, they prophesied, and did not cease… And Moses said unto him, Enviest thou for my sake? would God that all the Lord's people were prophets, and that the Lord would put his spirit upon them! Numbers 11:25&29**

There is a great anointing available to all those that are likeminded, or of the same blood type. The same blood type is important if there is to be a continual flow of the prophetic or the anointing of the intercessor. The church is God's vehicle of His divine presence. We are the vessels or channels of and for His divine flow in the earth. The church is called to act as one man, function as one man, and flow as one man.

Prophetic people are those who have a prophetic anointing for service. They don't have it on them at all times, yet when the anointing does come on them, it is for service. In order for you and I to wait on God, continually staying under the anointing, we must remain at the place of meditation, intercession, and prophetic influence. Just as you have a right and left hand, you have the gift of intercession and prophetic anointing on you, if you are a seer. To operate in one without the other, as a seer, is to operate using only one hand. To operate in the prophetic without being an intercessor is to operate using only one hand. It is important to understand that intercession is closely tied to the position of the seer, and the source of the prophetic power is found at that place of intimacy with their Father.

The prophetic flow of the seer is in seeing and not in speaking.

The prophet speaks from earth view. The seer speaks from an atmospheric view.

The seer speaks into the atmosphere because that's where the seer lives. The seer has to live at that particular place and level to see clearly everything he needs to see. The seer is concentrating only on one particular area of focus. The seer lives right where the Devil is. Someone has to be able to understand where the moves and the tricks of the Enemy reside. A lot of people think when the Devil got kicked out of heaven that he went to hell. He didn't go to hell, yet he fell down into the second heaven. God has planted some spies there who know what the Enemy is getting ready to do.

The prophet has his ear to the mouth of God, understanding every single thought, and intent of the heart of God, and everything that God wants to do. If we understand and see this in our spirit man, then we will understand clearly where the seer lives and why he lives there.

Understanding Regional Authority

The seer's authority is to look downward from the second heaven to see what the Devil is doing. From the seer's position of authority, he bombs his target.

The prophet lives in the third heaven, or dimension, in a place where he is able to see all the way down the road. Once the seer takes care of his assignment, this allows the prophet to speak forth to release into the atmosphere bringing about what God wants to change.

If the prophet, seer, and intercessor hear and obey, they will become a prophetic voice, clothed with that same prophetic anointing, speaking that same prophetic message. Why doesn't the church have the prophetic mantle on? The mantle is a type of vestment that is reserved for the office of the prophet. Therefore, one receives the mantle and the other receives an anointing that flows from the mantle.

The seer/intercessor, not the seer/prophet, is not necessarily qualified to bring the judgment as the prophet is qualified. When

NOTES

you bring something to the prophet because you saw something, you're not qualified to judge it. It is brought to the prophet because there is no cooperation, and it must be judged. The seer is qualified to dispense mercy.

As we go further, it is important that we see some other terms that will open our understanding clearly. The prophet's role in the earth is to speak into the lives of the people. Here is something to remember about roles:

The prophet. It is the assignment of the prophet to speak into the lives of the people to bring change. The prophet foretells and forth tells. None of the others are called to do those assignments.

The priest. The priest speaks to God on behalf of the people. This is so important to remember. Anyone who does not remember this will get out of order for sure. The prophet speaks to the people on the behalf of God; the priest speaks to God on behalf of the people.

The seer. The seer speaks to the leader on behalf of God regarding that which he sees at the present time. The seer does not say what he sees in the future; that part is reserved for the prophet.

The intercessor. The intercessor takes a stand between the people and God. God never desires to destroy the people; therefore, He puts in place an intercessor. Remember what He said in the Book of Ezekiel. God said, "I sought for a man among them who should stand in the gap and make up the hedge, but I found none." Remember that we talked about God's purpose being to create and destroy. That is exactly what will happen if there is not a shift and a type of Jesus who shows up to stand in the gap. There are a few examples of that I can think of. Moses was a person who prevented God from wiping out a whole nation of people by standing in the gap. Noah was another; by building an ark, a family of people and animals were saved. Abraham was another; a family was saved, except for Lot's wife, who looked back.

CHAPTER 5—Chapter Review

1. Before a prophet can come in and prophesy people into their destiny, what are the three things a seer/intercessor must do?

2. Define intercession. What is the difference between intercession and prophetic intercession?

3. Does a prophet serve in the role of intercession? If so, what is a prophet not permitted to do during intercession?

4. Discuss in detail the regional authority of the prophet and the seer.

5. Discuss in detail the roles of the prophet, the seer, the priest, and the intercessor. How are they similar? How do they differ?

CHAPTER 6—What Is an Apostle?

The term "apostle" may be defined and understood by the following terms and definitions:

Apostle: This word means "one sent." It is also defined as a specially commissioned messenger of the Lord, Jesus Christ. Apostles are granted, by God, plenipotentiary status in powers and delegated spherical principalities over which they rule. Apostles serve as Christ's stratospheric warriors and gubernatorial servants in the earth.

The apostles: The name for the twelve disciples of Christ elevated to the office of apostleship by Him during His earthly ministry. Their names were Simon Peter, Andrew, John, Philip, James, Bartholomew, Thomas, Matthew, Simon the Zealot, Jude, James and Judas Iscariot. Their ancient Hebrew counterpart is called "Shaliach." The basic meaning of this Hebrew term is "one sent from the Hebrew congregation, to let go or to send out." The shaliach was the personal representative of a sending person or group. He was also considered to be the legal representative of those who sent him. To conduct business with the shaliach was equivalent to conducting business face-to-face with the sender. These emissaries of the temple were dispatched and circulated to gather the tithes and offerings of the Diaspora and to disseminate temple teachings (Matt.10:1-5).

Apostolic: That which pertains to the apostle.

The Reestablishing of the Apostolic Office

As we look at the powerful thing the Lord has done in reestablishing the apostolic office, I think we will be amazed. God started with a wonderful order back in the fifties where He started putting together the evangelistic office. God has always pushed plurality of ministry. What that means is that there would be one visionary, but five leadership arms. If we are ever going to understand this, we must go back to the Book of Genesis.

In the beginning God (Elohim) created the heavens and the earth. Elohim is the word that expresses God in the plural sense. We dare not fight through this as whether God is one in three, or three in one. That is not the purpose of this teaching, nor do we discuss that subject in class. I want you to see the way God thinks and this pattern that God has. God has a pattern or habit of dealing in the plural sense of things. So in the beginning, Elohim created the heavens and the earth. Therefore, God will never leave plurality of ministry separated.

We are at that point now where God has restored all five of plurality of ministry. Next, in the sixties, God restored and magnified the office of the pastor. Pastors in that time were so magnified that we almost forgot that all of the other five ministry gifts existed but the two that had come forth at that time. We forgot that God was restoring all. So we saw only the pastor and the teacher for that decade.

During the seventies we saw much of the teaching ministry come to the forefront. It was at that time that the teachers' office was being magnified. Remember that every time God wants to bring attention to a certain office, He always magnifies it. Remember what happened when Moses died? God said to Joshua, *"This day will I begin to magnify thee in the sight of all Israel, that they may know that, as I was with Moses, so I will be with thee"* (Josh. 3:7). Therefore, God started to magnify the office of the teacher.

After that powerful decade of the teacher, we saw a tremendous move of God in the eighties of the prophet coming on the scene. The prophet was then magnified in the eyes of the people. That was a period when a tremendous challenge hit the body of Christ. Nevertheless, God was still in the business of magnifying and restoring that office.

As we think about those four offices that were restored back to the body of Christ, we have to see the negatives as well as the positives that were revealed. Nevertheless, God was still restoring it. In that decade, we saw many spiritual gifts turning on that at one point were lying dormant. That decade seemed to be a time when many in the body of Christ were revived to a point that probably looked like the decade of the fifties when the evangelist was being magnified and restored. The thing that both the prophet and the evangelist had in common was a powerful gift that had physical manifestation.

NOTES

The last office that had to be restored was that of the apostle. The apostle's office was also one of manifestation. One of the greatest tragedies that I saw within that period was the shifting between offices. There were pastors shifting to prophets and prophets shifting to apostles. One of the reasons for the seeming misidentification was that many who were in the office of pastors and shifted did not clearly understand that one could be a prophet and still flow in the office of a pastor. The same thing went for the apostle and prophet. There was just not enough information on the office.

So in the decade of the nineties, there was a lot of shifting going on. This was a shifting in place. We see now that we're in the twenty-first century and that there is still much shifting going on. This is because even though the fivefold offices are restored, there are still many who are just beginning to face the office to which they're really called.

Apostolic Confirmation: Extraordinary miracles/signs and wonders (2 Corinthians 12:12; Acts 4:30; 5:12; 16:30; 19:11; Romans 15:18-19; and Hebrews 2:4)

The apostle is an amazing person whom God has placed in the earth. There is so much information that we must understand about apostles. What are the characteristics of apostles? Do apostles exist today? What does God expect from apostles? How are apostles called? We will attempt to address these questions and more.

Paul, a servant of Jesus Christ, called to be an apostle, separated unto the gospel of God, (Which he had promised afore by his prophets in the Holy Scriptures,) Concerning his Son Jesus Christ our Lord, which was made of the seed of David according to the flesh; And declared to be the Son of God with power, according to the spirit of holiness, by the resurrection from the dead: By whom we have received grace and apostleship, for obedience to the faith among all nations, for his name: Among whom are ye also the called of Jesus Christ: Romans 1:1-6

44

In the previously mentioned passage of scripture, we find that Jesus Christ called Paul to be an apostle. In this time, we have witnessed many people, including those whom are called as apostles, who have just **gone** as opposed to having been **sent**. Paul was indeed called, but he had to wait on the sending. As an apostle, you don't just go because you know that you are called.

Recognizing Your Call

If you recognize your call as an apostle, there is no doubt that you will have to go through a tremendous season of training. Training is always necessary for the apostle as well as for the other ministry gifts.

Who has trained you as an apostle? Remember, Paul's declaration in 1 Corinthians 4:9-10,

> **For I think that God hath set forth us the apostles last, as it were appointed to death: for we are made a spectacle unto the world, and to angels, and to men. We are fools for Christ's sake, but ye are wise in Christ; we are weak, but ye are strong; ye are honorable, but we are despised. 1 Corinthians 4:9-10**

The apostle Paul clearly stated that apostles would be made into spectacles. If you will indeed be made into a spectacle, what example do you have that will guarantee your endurance of the test?

There are right and wrong ways to respond as you recognize your call. One of the greatest mistakes made by apostles is recognizing the call and failing to submit that call to their covering. If I am called as an apostle, it is imperative that I submit to the deepest degree of **submission.**

When the call is great, the submission has to be in proportion to that call. This is why Paul was able to say, "*But by the grace of God, I am what I am*" (1 Cor. 15:10).

Submission is always key in success in ministry. Paul recognized that it was not him, but the grace that was given to him that enabled him to be successful in ministry.

NOTES

For I am the least of the apostles, that am not meet to be called an apostle, because I persecuted the church of God. But by the grace of God I am what I am: and his grace which was bestowed upon me was not in vain; but I laboured more abundantly than they all: yet not I, but the grace of God which was with me. 1 Corinthians 15:9-10

For I speak to you Gentiles, inasmuch as I am the apostle of the Gentiles, I magnify mine office: Romans 11:13

It is also imperative that an apostle who has recognized his or her call clearly understand to whom he or she is called. It is not enough to know what you are called to do. Paul said, "I speak to you Gentiles, inasmuch as I am the apostle of the Gentiles." Paul understood exactly whom he was called to.

Apostles, like prophets, have regional authority. If you don't know the region you are called to, you can be found out of your lane and building where another person has been called. Therefore, the apostle must recognize what and to where he or she is called, but the responsibility is not limited to that. To whom are you called?

The Marks of a True Apostle

It is a good thing for us to know that a true apostle is marked by certain characteristics. Let's take a look at some of the things that Paul was challenged by, and we'll be able to see the marks and expectations that God has place upon apostles.

Mark #1—He or She Boasts in the Lord

Paul was growing in the Apostolic and came to the understanding that boasting was necessary, but it was not about to be profitable to him. In fact, the boasting was going to cause some major disadvantages for Paul. Nonetheless, he was going to do it because of those it *would* benefit.

It is not expedient for me doubtless to glory. I will come to visions and revelations of the Lord. 2 Corinthians 12:1 (KJV)

Boasting is necessary, though it is not profitable; but I will go on to visions and revelations of the Lord. 2 Corinthians 12:1 (NAS)

Mark #2—He or She Will Come to Visions and Revelations of the Lord

The apostle always arrives at the next level—at any cost. At this point, many people will stop short of what God has for them because of what they feel. Apostles, on the other hand, are not to stop short of anything.

Keep in mind that we don't permit ourselves to lead or to be led by the feeling realm. The feeling realm is where the Enemy deceives people and manipulates them out of the place where the delivery is designed to happen. The feeling realm is no place for the body of Christ to hang around because it is there that our Enemy has mastered his deceptive ways.

How do you know when you have entered the feeling realm? You know you are there when your "I feel like" or "I don't feel like" has become greater than your faith in what God said. Conversely, your thought process should be, "I will come into visions and revelations of the Lord. I will not allow my feelings to cheat me out of what I must have by coming short of God's expectations."

Mark #3—He or She Hears what He or She is Not Permitted to Speak

There are things the apostle hears from God that he or she will not be able to speak. Why, then, would God say things that he or she could not even speak or repeat? You are not to speak of everything that you hear. There are many things that God gives you for information's sake only. Jesus said, in the gospel of Saint John, "I have yet many things to say to you, but you can not bear them now."

How that he was caught up into paradise, and heard unspeakable words, which it is not lawful for a man to utter. 2 Corinthians 12:4 (KJV)

was caught up into Paradise and heard inexpressible words, which a man is not permitted to speak. 2 Corinthians 12:4 (NAS)

NOTES

47

God loves to reveal His mind to the apostle. Can you imagine how God feels when He is limited as to whom He can talk to on certain levels? Think what that must be like. You have things to talk about because your heart yearns for fellowship, not gossip-ship. Your heart is literally bursting with desire to share because you are so loaded with information, but you have no one with whom to share it. When God comes across an apostle like Paul who says, "I will come to visions and revelations of the Lord," I can imagine the expression on His face. I can see God as He raises His hand and arm up and pulls them down again as if He is ringing the church bell and shouting one big, "YES!"

Mark #4—He or She Always has a Thorn in His or Her Flesh

There is always an area in the life of an apostle that the Enemy buffets. This "thorn" keeps apostles mindful of the fact that the power is of God and not from them. What is it in your life that makes you remember that God is the reason for your living, moving, and having your being? When you think about what is happening in your life and the victories you are experiencing, what makes you point to God?

> **And lest I should be exalted above measure through the abundance of the revelations, there was given to me a thorn in the flesh, the messenger of Satan to buffet me, lest I should be exalted above measure. 2 Corinthians 12:7 (KJV)**

> **Because of the surpassing greatness of the revelations, for this reason, to keep me from exalting myself, there was given me a thorn in the flesh, a messenger of Satan to torment me—to keep me from exalting myself! 2 Corinthians 12:7 (NAS)**

I love the way Paul says, "the surpassing greatness of the revelations." What that says is that the revelations about which he speaks shoot far past anything else that God normally revealed to him. Jesus said, "I have yet many things to say to you, but you can't bear (handle) them now." Paul said, "My heart is enlarged towards you." And Moses covered his face because of the people's inability to handle what was on him or what he had experienced.

What would you do should you encounter "the surpassing greatness of the revelations"? As an apostle, would you be able to bear them now, would your heart be enlarged, or would you have to cover your face? Think about it.

Who is it that covers you? Can you handle the fullness of what God has placed in them? Can they unload the surpassing greatness of the revelations that God gave them to you? Probably not!

Mark #5—He or She Assumes Responsibility and Changes Circumstances Around Himself or Herself

Let's take a look at how the apostle Paul viewed his circumstances:

> **For this thing I besought the Lord thrice, that it might depart from me. And he said unto me, My grace is sufficient for thee: for my strength is made perfect in weakness. Most gladly therefore will I rather glory in my infirmities, that the power of Christ may rest upon me. 2 Corinthians 12:8-9 (KJV)**

> **Concerning this I implored the Lord three times that it might leave me. And He has said to me, "My grace is sufficient for you, for power is perfected in weakness." Most gladly, therefore, I will rather boast about my weaknesses, so that the power of Christ may dwell in me. 2 Corinthians 12:8-9 (NAS)**

This situation will truly challenge the person who wants someone else to kick in and do something about his or her situation. Paul, in this passage, looks to God and only God for help and for the removing of the thorn. But, God responds in a way in which Paul did not expect Him to respond. Paul was accustomed to God's rushing to his aid as God had done before the maturation stage. Once Paul came into the stage of maturity, God shifted the responsibility to Paul.

When you grow up, God no longer protects you the same way He used to. *Does* He protect you? Yes, but He does it differently. God no longer holds the sword that He used to protect you in times past. He gives it to you along with "how to" instructions.

49

Armed with his own sword, Paul was forced to look at his weaknesses differently. He proactively chose to glory in his weaknesses so that the power of Christ would rest upon him. What is that power of Christ? The Book of Philippians calls it *resurrection power*. For that reason, Paul declared, "… that I may know him and the power of His resurrection." Knowing the power of His resurrection brings us into greater ability.

I knew a man in Christ above fourteen years ago, (whether in the body, I cannot tell; or whether out of the body, I cannot tell: God knoweth;) such a one caught up to the third heaven. And I knew such a man, (whether in the body, or out of the body, I cannot tell: God knoweth;) How that he was caught up into paradise, and heard unspeakable words, which it is not lawful for a man to utter. Of such a one will I glory: yet of myself I will not glory, but in mine infirmities. For though I would desire to glory, I shall not be a fool; for I will say the truth: but now I forbear, lest any man should think of me above that which he seeth me to be, or that he heareth of me. And lest I should be exalted above measure through the abundance of the revelations, there was given to me a thorn in the flesh, the messenger of Satan to buffet me, lest I should be exalted above measure. 2 Corinthians 12:2-7 (KJV)

For this thing I besought the Lord thrice, that it might depart from me. And he said unto me, My grace is sufficient for thee: for my strength is made perfect in weakness. Most gladly therefore will I rather glory in my infirmities, that the power of Christ may rest upon me. Therefore I take pleasure in infirmities, in reproaches, in necessities, in persecutions, in distresses for Christ's sake: for when I am weak, then am I strong. I am become a fool in glorying; ye have compelled me: for I ought to have been commended of you: for in nothing am I behind the very chiefest apostles, though I be nothing. Truly the signs of an apostle were

wrought among you in all patience, in signs, and wonders, and mighty deeds. 2 Corinthians 12:8-12 (KJV)

Mark #6—He or She Flows in Extraordinary Signs, Wonders, and Miracles

The apostles always moved in signs and wonders. Jesus sent them out to do what He would have done by way of these supernatural workings. The apostles did not *hope* to do those things; they were *expected* to do them.

> **Truly the signs of an apostle were wrought among you in all patience, in signs, and wonders, and mighty deeds. 2 Corinthians 12:12 (KJV)**

> **The signs of a true apostle were performed among you with all perseverance, by signs and wonders and miracles. 2 Corinthians 12:12 (NAS)**

One could not call himself an apostle and not be able to make something happen. Bear in mind that as an apostle, you have had an encounter with God that has changed the way you look at God and yourself. Because you are associated with prophetic gifting, you have the freedom to operate in the revelation gifts. Therefore, signs and wonders are expected.

Mark #7—He or She is an Originator

I think it is vital to understand that the apostle does not build where others have already done a work. Apostles are those who go into places where no man has ever trod before. We, as a people, come after prophets or apostles, declaring a Word that has already been released into the atmosphere as if it were our own. We like to say what has already been said or build upon that which has already been built.

> **Yea, so have I strived to preach the gospel, not where Christ was named, lest I should build upon another man's foundation: But as it is written, To whom he was not spoken of, they**

NOTES

shall see: and they that have not heard shall understand. Romans 15:20-21 (KJV)

In this hour, God is looking for those who are ready to say what has not been said and to build what has not been built. God is looking for you and me to tread where people have not trodden before. We are the group that God can send to uninhabited places! We are to prepare a place of habitation for those that need such.

The apostle, along with the prophet, will dare to say the new thing or to introduce the unseen. In Matthew 10, Jesus sent the apostles into a place where He was not going to accompany them. Therefore, as an originator, you must understand that you are called to go to places where many will not go. You will see things in places that others won't see.

Mark #8—He or She Understands Divine Timing

Jesus says to this group of apostles, "Go not into the way of the Gentiles, and into any city of the Samaritans enter ye not." If we can understand that quote, we can understand that when we have an assignment, it may not be for now. God directed them to not go to the Gentiles or the Samaritans. They understood that if Jesus said that it was not time to go, then it was not time to go. Jesus did eventually go to the Syro-phonecian woman. He also went to the "woman at the well" who was from Samaria. Why would Jesus go to these women after telling the apostles not to go? The answer is simple: It was time. There are places that are time-sensitive. With this fact in mind, we must be conscious of this sensitivity. We cannot step out of time.

These twelve Jesus sent forth, and commanded them, saying, Go not into the way of the Gentiles, and into any city of the Samaritans enter ye not: But go rather to the lost sheep of the house of Israel. And as ye go, preach, saying, The kingdom of heaven is at hand. Matthew 10:5-7

None of the apostles, however, were called to the Gentiles. Ministering to the Gentiles was the apostle Paul's assignment.

Mark #9—He or She is a Spiritual Father

There are several powerfully anointed teachers and preachers within the body of Christ. Yet very few will subject themselves to the responsibility of spiritual fathering. This responsibility, however, is not a choice for the apostle. It is a necessity.

For though you have ten thousand instructors in Christ, yet have ye not many fathers: for in Christ Jesus I have begotten you through the gospel. 1 Corinthians 4:15

The apostle, like our Lord Jesus, will reproduce his ministry in others. Just as Jesus has entrusted and reproduced a portion of His ministry in every believer, apostles will likewise reproduce ministry in others.

As you have gathered from this teaching, the life and characteristics of an apostle are complex, yet recognizable. It is paramount that we know what an apostle is and how he or she functions so that the body of Christ may indeed be fitly joined together.

NOTES

CHAPTER 6—Chapter Review

1. In your own words, define what an apostle is.

2. What are the key elements in recognizing a call to the apostolic office?

3. Describe the marks of a true apostle.

CHAPTER 7—The Prophets' and Apostles' Call to Personal Balance

As prophets, we do most of our focusing on areas of the spirit. We are so spirit-focused that our natural relationships suffer. In this chapter, we focus on creating a balance in personal relationships. There are male prophets who rarely give attention to their wives. There are also female prophets who rarely give attention to their husbands. What does this create? This creates frustration in the home that spills over into the prophet's effectiveness in ministry. It is not possible for the prophet to be effective for a long period of time if home is not together. However, if home is together, there is a wonderful flow that spills over into ministry. One can pretend only for a short time.

Through God-given relationships, God has provided us with the power and ability that one needs to defeat the Enemy. Relationships have been there not to hinder us, but rather to protect us. If we can learn the purpose for which relationships were created, there will be no room for abuse. There are three facets of relationship that God has given us as a protective mechanism. The facets are prayer, worship, and the Word. Remember that God did certain things in threes. The three who bear record in heaven are the Father, Son, and the Holy Ghost. The three who bear witness in earth are the spirit, the water, and the blood. The triune protection of God is also threefold: God-ward relationship, brother and sister relationship, and spousal relationship.

God-ward Relationship

Your God-ward relationship is designed to bring you into a place of intimacy with God. Do you have a close relationship with God? The first person with whom we need to establish a relationship is God. Most of us are trying to fill needs and voids that only God can fill. God-ward relationship has three components that must be kept strong. Keep these three areas strong so the Enemy will not come through the cracks. The three areas are:

- Prayer—Your communication with God
- Worship—Your yielding to God
- Word—Your direction in God

The first component is "prayer." God-ward relationship is God's plan to bring you into a healthy place. People go after psychics because they do not have a prayer life! God is trying to get you to a place of prayer.

The second component is "worship." Worship means coming into an intimate place with God. Many people are trying to enter into a place of intimacy by trying to be with this person or that person, but there is an actual hunger on the inside of them so much that they are unable to see what God has for them. God is pulling on them, but because they have something else in their view, they will go after it instead of going after God and this place call worship. You must understand why you have this strong desire to be intimate. The first thing that many of us do is look for a woman or a man. **God is saying that you will not find it in them, but in Him! He needs you to come closer to Him!**

The third component is the "Word." God then leads us into the Word for direction. The Word of God will get you out of your problems.

Brother and Sister Relationship

This relationship is designed to do three things for you and in you. Many times we try to get around relationships such as this kind because we think that we are not in direct need of that brother or sister. I have three questions to ask you. To whom are you accountable? With whom do you commune? With whom are you so in love? We actually need that brother or sister to sharpen us in three areas. Those three areas are:

- Love—Agape (unconditional) and Phileo (brotherly)
- Communion —Koinonia or fellowship
- Accountability—Being responsible or liable to someone

Agape Love

Unconditional love is what God want us to have in this pure brother and sister relationship. We must know where to draw the line in this brother-to-brother and sister-to-sister relationship. This relationship is one where we enter a place of love with them, but it is agape love. Often we come to a place in our relationship with

56

a brother or sister where God never intended for it to go. As a result, it becomes perverted love.

Phileo or brotherly love

God has no problem with a brother-to-brother, a brother-to-sister, a sister-to-sister, or a sister-to-brother relationship, as long you know where to draw the line. **Keep it pure!**

Koinonia or fellowship

This is a relationship in which you actually commune with your brother or sister.

Accountability

We may have the love and communion together, but we do not always have the accountability together because it means that we must become responsible or liable for someone. Who is it that corrects you, or have you set up yourself to be corrected by anyone? **You should have a brother or sister who will put you in check!** God established that brother and sister relationship so that we can be accountable to someone. **Understand this: You can't tell everybody your stuff.**

These are qualities that one needs to possess in relationship to our brother and sister. It will mean the difference between your being married or not married.

Spousal Relationship

When you are in the brother and sister relationship, there is a very important facet that enhances your ability to be committed to your spouse. This facet is "accountability." If you are unable to be accountable to a brother or sister, then you will never be able to exemplify the kind of commitment that God is looking for in a marriage. What about communion in a marriage? How many husbands or wives do we know who cannot talk to each other? Your spouse should be your best friend. If he or she is not, then you are at a very vulnerable place! Are you on your way to marriage? If you are in a relationship with someone who is not your best friend now, then that person will not be your best friend later. **You must be able to commune with the other person!** This relationship is

NOTES

the act of sharing one's intimate thoughts and emotions with another person.

God gives us the brother-to-brother or sister-to-sister relationship so that we may go to the next level of relationship. Make sure that you have in place the God-ward relationship, the brother and sister relationship, and the spousal relationship. The reason for the relationships is so that we can stay at a committed place with God, a committed place with a brother or sister, and a committed place with our spouse.

CHAPTER 7—Chapter Review

1. Name the three facets of relationship God has given us as protective mechanisms.

2. Describe the function and purpose of the God-ward relationship.

3. Describe the function and purpose of the brother and sister relationship.

4. Describe the function and purpose of the spousal relationship.

SEASON #2
SEASON OF CHALLENGED PURPOSE

chal lenge
n. ME & OFr *chalenge*, accusation, claim, dispute < L *calumnia*, CALUMNY
1 a demand for identification [a sentry gave the *challenge*]
2 a calling into question; a demanding of proof, explanation, etc.[a *challenge* of the premises of an argument]
3 a call or dare to take part in a duel, contest, etc.
4 anything, as a demanding task, that calls for special effort or dedication
5 an objection to a vote or to someone's right to vote
6 *Law* a formal objection or exception to a person who has been chosen as a prospective juror

—taken from *Webster's New World Dictionary*

There is a season that the prophet goes through when he or she is challenged to see what level of pressure he or she is able to handle. If the prophet is unable to handle pressure in this season, he or she is disqualified for his or her readiness for the next season.

No one just goes to the next season. There has to be a qualifying process. You must be made ready for what is next. Notice our definition of "challenge." Through this season there will be accusation, claim, and dispute. The question is, Can you handle those kinds of things? Remember, you are called and anointed to solve problems. In the season of challenge, you learn these kinds of things, but only if you are a catcher. If the best you can do is learn from lessons taught verbally, then the season of challenge will defeat you. The season of challenge is a season during which you learn to catch lessons more than being verbally taught them. Some things are taught; other things are caught. The season of challenge is a catching season.

Being accused is the norm in this season. Accusation is not something that is designed to kill you, but to grow you. Many of these kinds of opportunities come to us as prophets and apostles, but we forfeit the growth by not allowing it to work for us.

NOTES
_____
_____
_____
_____
_____
_____
_____
_____
_____
_____
_____
_____
_____
_____
_____
_____

"For our light affliction, which is but for a moment, worketh for us a far more exceeding and eternal weight of glory; While we look not at the things which are seen, but at the things which are not seen: for the things which are seen are temporal; but the things which are not seen are eternal." 2 Corinthians 4:17-18

The thing we must master is that there are things that work for us, but the criterion is, "We look not at what is seen, but at what is not seen." Let the season of challenge work for you a far more exceeding weight of glory.

CHAPTER 8—Understanding the Father–Son Relationship

Father–Son Relationship From an Earthly Perspective

The concept of the father–son relationship has been widely misunderstood. The misunderstanding of this vitally important relationship has surfaced in part because of the earthly perspective from which we've drawn our understanding.

The concept of fathering did not originate from an earthly pattern; yet, when we think of the spiritual father or the spiritual son, we confine our thinking to earthly models that we have either observed or experienced. This earthly perspective of the father–son relationship causes us to experience difficulties and conflicts when we attempt to initiate and maintain spiritual father–son relationships from this perspective. We have made the concept of the father–son relationship too earthly.

From an earthly perspective, we are governed by gender-based assignments. Gender-based assignments require a male and female in order to produce a son. In other words, if I have a father, I must also have a mother. Therefore, if I am to have a spiritual father, I must also have a spiritual mother. Moreover, if we attach gender to the spiritual father–son relationship, we must deal with some very important questions: Who was the mother of Jesus? Who was the father of Jesus? Who was the mother of Christ? Who was the father of Christ? As we think in differentiating terms such as *Jesus* and *Christ*, it is imperative that we separate earthly from heavenly. Jesus is who made Christ legal in the earth in the same manner that "ish" made Adam legal in the earth. Likewise, your physical body is what makes you legal in the earth. If it was not for your physical body, you would not be legal in the earth, nor would you be able to remain in the earth.

When Jesus stepped down from His holy habitation to become the Word manifested in flesh, did He need a spiritual mother to make Himself complete, or was He complete before He actually took His first step on His way to earth? The answer to both questions is, "Certainly not!" Jesus was already complete. His state of completeness was never contingent upon whether or not He had a spiritual mother. Jesus was and is complete in God. Let's prove

NOTES

this point by recalling to memory the question Jesus posed as recorded in the book of Luke: *"How is it that ye sought me? wist ye not that I must be about my Father's business?"* (Luke 2:49). What father was Jesus talking about—His earthly or heavenly father? This question that Jesus posed at the young age of twelve proves that He was, indeed, complete in God.

It must be understood that when God deals with sonship, He does not deal with gender. If we deal with the father–son relationship from an earthly perspective, we find the previously asked questions very difficult to answer as they pertain to this type of relationship. If we, however, deal with the father–son relationship from a heavenly perspective, we find God to be our ALL. The concept of the father–son relationship from a heavenly perspective shows us that fathering is not based upon gender but upon the pattern of our heavenly father, who is and has become all to us.

Sonship, as we know it to be defined in the earth, requires both a mother and a father. This definition is supported by science, which teaches that the creation of a human requires an egg and a sperm. Biology professors have aptly taught us that life or conception necessitates the deposit and uniting of a man's sperm with a woman's egg. In simpler terms, children can be born only with the cooperation of two separate entities: a man and a woman. That's how children are formed; they receive their total genetic makeup from two separate contributions—one from the male (father) and one from the female (mother). Subsequently, it becomes commonplace for us to believe that every son—natural or spiritual—must have both a father and mother. This is, in a nutshell, an earthly perspective.

The heavenly perspective, or God's perspective, is vastly different. While it takes both father and mother in order to properly develop children in the natural, this is true only from an earthly perspective. In contrast, from the heavenly perspective, or God's perspective, God deposits **everything** you, as a son, need into your spiritual father. All that you need to become whom God created you to be is wrapped up on the inside of your spiritual father. God's pattern of fathering does not require a spiritual mother.

The term "spiritual mother" has been used primarily because of our misunderstanding of the spiritual father concept and our enslavement to gender directives. When it comes to fathering, God is simply not concerned with gender. The Bible states the following:

For as many as are led by the Spirit of God, they are the sons of God. Romans 8:14

If the Word of God is true, and it is, then being a spiritual *"son"* has nothing at all to do with gender. This clearly seen principle rings true not only for spiritual sons, but for spiritual fathers. Gender can't be attached to spiritual fathering in the earth. Therefore, the set gift or spiritual father may be male or female. However, if a pastor/set gift is a female, she may have biological children but does not automatically become a spiritual mother to her biological children. Just as God has given to the male pastors/set gifts everything that their spiritual sons will need to reach their destiny, so He does with the female pastors/set gifts. "Female" is the package she comes in; "Father" is what is inside of the package.

What do you do with the birthing process if you are not going to deal with the father–son relationship from an earthly perspective? Dealing with the father–son relationship from an earthly perspective and excluding gender causes us to revisit the Genesis account:

> **And God said, Let us make man in our image, after our likeness: and let them have dominion over the fish of the sea, and over the fowl of the air, and over the cattle, and over all the earth, and over every creeping thing that creepeth upon the earth. Genesis 1:26**

The word "man" in this passage is derived from the Hebrew word "Adam," which is defined as "person" or "mankind." The word "Adam" can also refer to male or female (*The Hebrew Greek Study Bible*). In this writing, the term for man is referred to as one who was created, while the term "man" in Genesis 2:23, which is *"ish"—a masculine noun that distinguishes male from female—* refers to one who was made. Simply stated, we are discussing nothing less than the male, husband, mate, or male man. On the other hand, the word *"neqevah"* means *"woman or female whether human or animal."* The fact that this word is associated with the words "female," "woman," or "animal" confirms that it is an earthly term that answers to gender as opposed to a heavenly term that is not gender-specific and answers to God. If we choose to think in heavenly terms, we must drive out earthly terms. "Heav-

65

enly" has no gender attached to it. "Earthly" has gender attached to it. If we look past gender, we will be able to see the father–son relationship as God sees it. For example:

> **There is neither Jew nor Greek, there is neither bond nor free, there is neither male nor female: for ye are all one in Christ Jesus. And if ye be Christ's, then are ye Abraham's seed, and heirs according to the promise. Galatians 3:28-29**

This scripture refers to the heavenly or non-gender idea. It basically tells us that the son could be either male or female. Likewise, the father could be either male or female. Anytime you think that a father or a son could be male or female, you must realize that you are not dealing from an earthly perspective. In turn, if you are dealing with the thought that the gender makeup of a bride could either be male or female, you must—again—realize that you are not dealing from an earthly perspective. If we are dealing with *"ish"* (man) or *"neqevah"* (woman), then we are dealing from the earthly perspective and not the heavenly perspective.

To aid us in our understanding of the father–son relationship, we must think in third-dimension terms as opposed to second-dimension terms. There are a lot of things that don't exist in the third dimension that we have grown accustomed to in the second dimension. When we deal with earthly perspectives and groom ourselves to think solely in terms of earthly matters, God will admonish us as He did the Colossians:

> **If ye then be risen with Christ, seek those things which are above, where Christ sitteth on the right hand of God. Set your affection on things above, not on things on the earth. Colossians 3:1-2**

This verse begins by saying *"if ye then be risen,"* indicating that it is possible that we could have a different concept or understanding than the author does. But if we are indeed risen, then we have to think on different terms. The terms that God suggests that we think on will require us to shift in our thinking and where we set our affections. Think on **things above**, and **set your affection on things above, not on things on the earth.** Accomplishing this is going to call for a total transformation in our thought patterns. When we understand this, we will understand why we must embrace the father–son relationship from the heavenly perspective.

Father–Son Relationship From a Heavenly Perspective

Many believers in the body of Christ are experiencing difficulties in embracing the father–son relationship. Much of the difficulty they experience is a direct result of the perspective they employ while considering the father–son relationship. The concept of the father–son relationship is not based upon an earthly understanding. If we try to exist in a spiritual father–son relationship based upon an earthly perspective, we will encounter an immeasurable amount of frustration and confusion. The father–son relationship, although it has been widely misunderstood within Christendom, originated from God and can be comprehended only by adopting a heavenly perspective.

Naturally, when we think of a "fathering" relationship, we automatically consider gender. "Only men can be fathers." Well, this holds true in society, where there are gender boundaries, rightly set, in the earth. Because we are earthbound, when we think of fathering relationships, what generally comes to mind is the many examples of fathers we have seen in the earth. However, when we regard a spiritual "fathering" relationship, the only example of a father that we need to look to is our heavenly father. Fortunately, God has established the heavenly pattern for the earthbound spiritual father to follow.

In order to understand the concept of the father–son relationship from a heavenly perspective, certain components need to be in place so that this relationship can operate at its fullest potential, yielding benefits to both the father and the son.

The first component that we will examine in the father–son relationship is the teknon component.

The Teknon Component

In John 1, the apostle wrote: *"But as many as received him, to them gave he power to become the sons* [teknon] *of God, even to them that believe on his name:"* (John 1:12). The Greek word for sons in this passage is "teknon." This word for son indicates that the person or persons spoken of are sons by birth. The teknon stage is the first stage, where a son actually reaches in the father–son relationship. It is a phase where, although he is a son, he has not reached full development. At this point, his features, although maturing, are not yet distinct. The "teknon" son may vaguely resemble the father; however, upon first glance, he is not immediately recognized as the son of his father. Further maturation and character development are needed. Yet, he is **still** a son.

The Huios Component

"Huios" is another Greek word for son and is used throughout the New Testament. This word is best exemplified when Paul exhorts the Corinthians to be followers of Him. As a "huios," following or imitating, as another biblical version translates, is what the "huios" son does best. Unlike the "teknon" component of sonship, the "huios" component of sonship requires action. At the "huios" stage of sonship, the son displays marked and distinct features revealing that he is indeed the son of his father. Unlike the "teknon" stage, this word for son indicates that the son is a son of character. "Elder, you act just like the pastor. You even say the same things he says. I'll tell you, if I weren't looking in your face I would've sworn that I had heard Bishop speaking." In the huios phase, the son takes on all of the characteristics of his father. He says what his father says, does what his father does, and acts as his father acts. Contrary to the "teknon" stage, this phase of sonship can be attained only by purposeful pursuit. The "huios" son is a son on purpose.

The Responsibility Component

Genesis 18, which details the patriarch Abraham and his angelic encounter, gives us a great outline of the responsibility component of sonship. Let us review some of the son's responsibilities—submission, obedience, and reciprocity:

Submission

> **And he lift up his eyes and looked, and lo, three men stood by him: and when he saw them, he ran to meet them from the tent door, and bowed himself toward the ground, Genesis 18:2**

As Abraham bowed himself to the ground, he placed himself

at the disposal of the angels, showing he had no defense. He was in a posture of total submission. In order to have a successful father–son relationship, the son must find himself revisiting the place of submission frequently.

Obedience

> **And I will fetch a morsel of bread, and comfort ye your hearts; after that ye shall pass on: for therefore are you come to your servant. And they said, So do, as thou hast said. And Abraham hastened....Genesis 18:5-6**

After declaring what he *would* do, the angels commanded him to do as he said. If you continue reading on, you will notice that Abraham **hastened.** Not only was Abraham obedient, he was quick to be obedient. Sons must hasten to be obedient. If you believe, as a son, that you must analyze and critique every command that your father gives, perhaps sonship and its fruit are not for you—and being an illegitimate son is.

Reciprocity

> **And they said unto him, Where is Sarah thy wife? And he said, Behold, in the tent. And he said, I will certainly return unto thee according to the time of life; and lo, Sarah thy wife shall have a son... Genesis 18:9-10**

How is it that reciprocity is considered to be a son's responsibility?

In the first eight verses of this chapter, Abraham is found serving to his heart's content. Abraham ran to meet the angels from the tent door, fetched their water, washed their feet, fetched them bread, and fetched a tender calf for them, providing the angels with a tasty meal underneath the tree. What a servant! Now, Abraham's hour of reciprocity was nigh. It was his responsibility, in order to receive the reciprocal blessing, to be in place. As sons, each of our blessings has been addressed to our homes or dwelling places. Our homes, such as they are, have been addressed ac-

NOTES

cording to our lineage or line of succession. Your blessing will be sent only to the place that bears the name of your father. It is your responsibility to be at home and in place.

The Vulnerability Component

The son has the responsibility of willingly making himself vulnerable to his father. It is said of Timothy, *"Him would Paul have to go forth with him; and took and circumcised him..."* (Acts 16:3). Circumcision is the test of a true son. Successful circumcision requires total trust on the son's behalf. During this delicate procedure, the son must willingly bare all of his most private parts—to a man. He is not able to leave even the smallest portion of "his stuff" covered. All areas must be exposed to this man he calls his "spiritual father." In addition, the son must trust that his father has a steady and skillful hand as the procedure dictates. Should the son demonstrate even an iota of distrust, it is possible that what was intended to be a sign of covenant would result in an incidence of castration. Sons must allow themselves to trust their fathers, even to the point of self-exposure.

The Covenant Component

Covenant is one of the most sacred components in a relationship. It is what binds one person with another, one heart to another. Adam made an awesome pronouncement as he declared and ratified his covenantal relationship with his wife. Adam spoke these words regarding Eve: *"This is now bone of my bones, and flesh of my flesh:..."* (Gen. 2:23). The concept of a father–son relationship from a heavenly perspective calls for covenant. Believe it or not, we are recognized from heaven based upon our covenantal relationships. For example, after fleeing from the face of her mistress, Hagar is accosted by an angel of the Lord by the fountain in the way of Shur. The angel asks her, *"Hagar, Sarai's maid, whence camest thou?..."* (Gen. 16:8) Notice that he didn't address her as Hagar Smith, or Hagar, the girl from Kenilworth, but she was recognized from heaven by her covenantal relationship in the earth. This account accurately describes how sons are recognized in heaven—by their spiritual covenantal relationships in the earth. Without a daddy, you don't even have a name.

The Blessing Component

This component of the father–son relationship applies exclusively to the spiritual father. It is the responsibility of the father to bless the son, provided the son has done what is required of him to be blessed. When the father pronounces the blessing over the son, the words that he speaks sprout legs and arms. These words now become agents with the assignment to unlock every door and to release every promise into the hands of the son. The power these words possess to unlock doors and to release promises is not found solely in the words themselves but in the position and authority of the father.

Learning to Father Leaders

Before anyone can function as a father or a type of father, they must submit themselves under the hand of someone else on earth. There are times when the person to whom you need to submit may seem to be less capable than you, yet God still has you submit under their hand.

There was a time when Jesus, becoming ready for ministry, had one more person to whom He had to submit aside from the one that posed as his natural father (Joseph). The person to whom He submitted after leaving Joseph was John the Baptist at the baptism. John the Baptist felt very much incapable of baptizing Him, and he bears this out by saying, *"I have need to be baptized of thee"* (Matt. 3:14). That was the point when Jesus humbled Himself and submitted under the hand of John. He went from there to the wilderness to be tempted and to go through his period of being tried.

Jesus returned from the wilderness and began the selection of his sons for ministry. Yes, He Himself hand-picked his own sons that He would pour into. The interesting thing about handpicking His own sons is that some had to leave their natural fathers and come under the authority of their spiritual father. Until we come under the authority of our spiritual father, we will never be able to function in the position as a son. There must be absolute submission under a father.

Let's look at some major details about their father–son relationship.

71

NOTES

_____

_____

_____

_____

_____

_____

_____

_____

_____

_____

_____

_____

_____

_____

Now when Jesus had heard that John was cast into prison, he departed into Galilee; And leaving Nazareth, he came and dwelt in Capernaum, which is upon the sea coast, in the borders of Zabulon and Nephthalim: That it might be fulfilled which was spoken by Esaias the prophet, saying, the land of Zabulon, and the land of Nephthalim, by the way of the sea, beyond Jordan, Galilee of the Gentiles; The people which sat in darkness saw great light; and to them which sat in the region and shadow of death light is sprung up. From that time Jesus began to preach, and to say, Repent: for the kingdom of heaven is at hand. Matthew 4:12-17

And Jesus, walking by the sea of Galilee, saw two brethren, Simon called Peter, and Andrew his brother, casting a net into the sea: for they were fishers. And he saith unto them, Follow me, and I will make you fishers of men. And they straightway left their nets, and followed him. And going on from thence, he saw other two brethren, James the son of Zebedee, and John his brother, in a ship with Zebedee their father, mending their nets; and he called them. And they immediately left the ship and their father, and followed him. And Jesus went about all Galilee, teaching in their synagogues and preaching the gospel of the kingdom, and healing all manner of sickness and all manner of disease among the people. Matthew 4:18-23

1. Leaving Your Comfort Zone and Place of Support, v. 12

Jesus left the comfort of Nazareth, where He was raised, along with his family support and all that He cared about and loved. He came to a place that, later on, He would have to weep over because they hadn't grasped their time of visitation. This is a place where every father and every son have to meet. It's what I call a place of surrender and a place of abandonment. This place is a strange place where there is no moral support or spiritual support, only nothingness. This is that type of place that will cause many to wonder why you left and wonder what purpose could there possibly be for going to a place such as Capernaum. Every father must learn to exist where there is nothing but surrender. Every son must come to a place with a father where there is nothing to do but surrender and sit at his feet. There is great power at the feet of a master teacher for the son if he only learns to wait.

2. Shining for or in Another Man's Dream, v. 16

Jesus, at this point, realizes that His only position is to shine for another man's purpose. As a son, it is imperative that we understand that unless we shine for another man's dream, we'll never see the fulfillment of our own dreams. As we understand this very important position, we'll also understand the way to fatherhood. The ultimate is to become a father and not remain only a son. We find later that the disciples (sons) were called by Jesus (father) to shine in His dream, which was to reach the lost at all cost. My question to you is: "Are you trying to shine for yourself when you have been called into another man's dream?" If you are, your dream can never be realized because you are trying to shine in your dream when yours has never died.

3. Preaching Another Man's Word, v. 17

It is amazing to me that Jesus came preaching the same Word that John the Baptist preached. Remember that Jesus submitted Himself under the hand of John the Baptist and never showed Himself until John the Baptist was going off the scene. A son can never show himself until the father is going off the scene. There is a problem in our society today. We, as sons, are trying to show ourselves before our father has gone off the scene. John the Baptist, being a type of a father in this case, was not dead, but just off the scene. It is not necessary for your father to be dead, but it is necessary for him to be off the scene. Note also that it is important to always stay in a submitted position under your father until he comes to a place of nonexistence. This marks the time for your arising. The real test of whether your time has come is how well you speak your father's word. There will always be an increase of knowledge and revelation that may supersede what your father has said, but it is only likely to happen after he ceases to exist. His death becomes your rising.

NOTES

73

4. Locating Your Sons, vv. 18-19

At this point, Jesus starts the process of locating His sons, who will function as His staff. God always causes a father to locate sons, or staff. Not only does God cause a father to locate his sons, but He also causes him to place his spirit on his sons in order to reproduce what he has been made as a father. There is a word that comes to mind when I, as a father, think of a son or daughter. I have the awesome challenge to duplicate myself in them and to say what Jesus said, *"Follow me, and I will make you fishers of men."* The condition of a son is to "follow me." Any son who has a problem following the father (leader) forfeits the benefit of having a portion of that father. The word "follow" is extremely important to having portion of your father's spirit. This means you must follow at all cost. Sometimes the cost is great and sometimes not so great. At any rate, there is a cost to capturing the spirit of your father.

The benefit of following is "I will make you." The making comes during the process of following. The word "following" is progressive, is continuous, and illustrates a method of not stopping the said action. The making happens as you continue following. Some have forfeited their making because they ceased in their following. Now, we return to the prerequisite, *"Follow me, and I will make you fishers of men."*

I will make you that which I am. God told Moses to choose seventy elders who were faithful, of a good report, and full of wisdom. Although the elders (sons) had those qualities, God said there was still something lacking. They had great gifting and great qualities, yet the missing ingredient to activate all of that greatness was the spirit of their father. God said to Moses, "You choose the men and I will take of the spirit upon thee and will put it upon them." (Num. 11:16-17) The spirit that God was referring to within the context of this scripture would be equivalent to the anointing that was smeared upon Moses.

5. Leaving the Natural Father and Cleaving to the Spiritual Father, v. 20

It was a custom for the natural father to teach natural hobbies and abilities. The spiritual father was the one who had the challenge to impart spiritual gifts.

CHAPTER 8—Chapter Review

1. Describe the difference between the earthly and heavenly perspective as it pertains to gender. Provide scripture to support your description.

2. Define teknon.

3. Define huios.

4. Describe the responsibility component of sonship.

5. What is one of the most important prerequisites for functioning as a father or type of father in the earth?

CHAPTER 9—The Purpose of the Prophet

The prophet is multifaceted in both operation and assignment. If the prophet is not careful to remain and to operate within his particular assignment, he will waiver and never fulfill his purpose. What is the prophet's assignment? The prophet's assignment is:

To Locate Lost Children

> **Behold, I will send you Elijah the prophet before the coming of the great and dreadful day of the Lord: And he shall turn the heart of the fathers to the children, and the heart of the children to their fathers, lest I come and smite the earth with a curse." Malachi 4:5-6**

It is important to note that we, as prophets—even senior prophets—have the assignment of locating lost children. In this hour when God is revealing or exposing bastards, it is imperative that the prophet locate lost children so that the children's hearts can be turned to their fathers and so that the curse can be eliminated.

In addition, prophets must be mindful to turn the hearts of the children to **their** fathers. We must not overlook the possessive pronoun "their." Prophets should never desire someone else's children but should always send the children back to **their** fathers.

We (as set gifts) often make the mistake of calling ourselves someone's father simply because they are our members. This is not always the case. Just because they are members does not make them children, nor does it make us fathers. We may **not** be their fathers. In fact, we may only be *"instructors"* to them (1 Cor. 4:15). Once we understand where we are, we must begin the process of turning the children's hearts back to **their** fathers.

As an addendum to the assignment to locate lost children, the task of relocating lost children is also extremely important. As prophets, we have been given the awesome responsibility to minister to those persons who have been misplaced or displaced. Many prophets and prophetic people fail to understand the magnitude of their responsibility. For the most part, we think that when we come into the knowledge of people's information or when we are able to observe that people are out of place, we think that these things have taken place simply by chance.

Many prophets and prophetic people have come into contact with people who have been disjointed from local churches, from men and women of God, and are now wavering throughout the body of Christ. This is not abnormal. In fact, because it is very normal, we have come to take these occurrences for granted.

Sadly, when we become so accustomed to a particular way of doing things, we almost don't know where to go to in a given situation, so we end up in the same system that killed us the last time. The Book of Deuteronomy provides a solution for this:

> **Break camp and advance into the hill country of the Amorites; go to all the neighboring peoples in the Arabah, in the mountains, in the western foothills, in the Negev and along the coast, to the land of the Canaanites and to Lebanon, as far as the great river, the Euphrates. Deuteronomy 1:7 (NIV)**

Let's keep the words "*break camp and advance*" in perspective. Just because you feel as if you're dying doesn't always mean that we need to break camp. To a degree, God wants to kill you. **He** wants to live. There is a clear sign in the Word of God that defines for us a time when God wants to kill us:

> **For thou hast said in thine heart, I will ascend into heaven, I will exalt my throne above the stars of God: I will sit also upon the mount of the congregation, in the sides of the north: I will ascend above the heights of the clouds; I will be like the most High. Yet thou shalt be brought down to hell, to the sides of the pit. Isaiah 14:13-17 (KJV)**

> **Anytime we have that many I's, we must endure an amount of dying.**

Knowing when to exit the system is paramount to your spiritual life. Most of us are afraid of the "different." As prophets and

NOTES

77

prophetic people, we are going to have to tap into something different. The next move of God is going to be different. It will not be something that we are accustomed to.

We must guard ourselves from remaining in the same system and endeavor to come to advancement *in God*—to a place where we have increased—to a place where we can declare, "Well, that was one period in my life where I realize I am not the same person I used to be." This knowledge and declaration will bring them to a place where they will occupy their God-ordained position in the body of Christ.

To Pour Into Sons and Daughters

Joel 2:28, Psalm 133:1-3; 1 Samuel 10:5-13

> **And it shall come to pass afterward, that I will pour out my spirit upon all flesh; and your sons and your daughters shall prophesy, your old men shall dream dreams, your young men shall see visions: Joel 2:28**

When we discuss pouring into sons and daughters, we must consider the heavenly perspective. The prophet Joel prophesied of a time when God would pour out His Spirit on all flesh and that sons and daughters would prophesy. What is needed to prophesy? Oil! Do you have the oil necessary to prophesy? If so, is the oil that you're operating from legitimate or stolen? How can you tell the difference? Let's look at Psalm 133:

> **Behold, how good and how pleasant it is for brethren to dwell together in unity. It is like the precious ointment upon the head, that ran down upon the beard, even Aaron's beard: that went to the skirts of his garments; As the dew of Hermon, and as the dew that descended upon the mountains of Zion: for there the Lord commanded the blessing, even life for evermore. Psalm 133:1-4**

We notice in this passage of scripture that the oil runs from the head downward. It runs from the head of Aaron down to the beard of Aaron. It then runs down on the edge of Aaron's gar-

78

ments. If you are positioned properly, you will have **legitimate** oil upon you.

The type of oil that will flow down to you will depend upon the oil of the house. For example, if the set gift is a prophet, then the house is prophetic, and prophetic oil will run down. If the set gift is an apostle, then the house is apostolic, and apostolic oil will run down. If you are a properly positioned evangelist, submitted to a set gift who is a prophet, and you are a member of his house, you are now an evangelist with prophetic oil. Keep in mind that the oil **does not change the office**; however, **it will change the man**. We can see a perfect example of this in 1 Samuel 10:5-13:

> **"After that you shall come to the hill of God where the Philistine garrison is. And it will happen, when you have come there to the city, that you will meet a group of prophets coming down from the high place with a stringed instrument, a tambourine, a flute, and a harp before them; and they will be prophesying. Then the Spirit of the Lord will come upon you, and you will prophesy with them and be turned into another man.... And it happened, when all who knew him formerly saw that he indeed prophesied among the prophets, that the people said to one another, "What is this that has come upon the son of Kish? Is Saul also amongst the prophets?" 1 Samuel 10:5-6 & 11 (NKJV)**

To Declare and to Create

> **Then God said, "Let Us make man in Our image, according to Our likeness; let them have dominion over the fish of the sea, over the birds of the air, and over the cattle, over all the earth and over every creeping thing that creeps on the earth." So God created man in His own image; in the image of God He created him; male and female He created them. Then God blessed them, and God said to them, "Be fruitful and multiply; fill the earth and subdue it; have dominion over the fish of the sea, over**

NOTES

79

the birds of the air, and over every living thing that moves on the earth." Genesis 1:26-28 (NKJV)

If you don't have dominion, you won't create anything.

As prophets, we are the mouthpieces of God. Prophets must learn to declare and create things in the same manner in which God did. God spoke and things became. God declared a thing to be, and the thing was created. Prophets not only have this same ability, but they also have the assignment to do likewise. God desires that we declare and create things through and by our words, coupled with the prophetic ability we possess on the inside. We must properly understand our position as prophets so that when we begin to declare and create, we're not just saying something.

Because of this prophetic ability, prophets and prophetic people tend to have, more than anyone else, problems with gossip. The reason is simple: Satan will do anything in his power to get you to violate your position so that God will be unable to reveal things to you. Shut your eyes to any information that you're not authorized to carry. Do not even desire to know the information. Do not even concern yourself with it. Avoid it.

Gossip is unauthorized information carried by an individual who is not authorized to carry that information.

In addition, because we have the ability to declare and create, we must stay away from "death statements" in order to express ourselves such as "I laughed to death" and "I love you to death."

If you continue to use these kinds of words, whether in conversation or song, God will be unable to release to you the level of authority you need in your words to declare and create because you've failed to understand the power of words. It is necessary that you be conscious of your words.

For verily I say unto you, That whosoever shall say unto this mountain, Be thou removed, and be thou cast into the sea; and shall not doubt in his heart, but shall believe that those things

which he saith shall come to pass; he shall have whatsoever he saith. Mark 11:23

Notice, in the above-mentioned scripture, that the word "say" (or its form) was mentioned three times, and "believe" was mentioned only once. It is clear that you can have what you say. The key to having what you say is declaring and creating from both your heart and mouth. Romans 10:8 asks:

But what saith it? The word is nigh thee, even in thy mouth, and in thy heart: that is, the word of faith, which we preach; Romans 10:8

When we insist upon making "death statements," we have to realize that these statements are made from both our mouths and our hearts.

It is also our responsibility to make deposits into people, provoking them to understand that they can say a thing and that thing will be.

Jesus understood this as He made a deposit in the onlookers found in John 11:39-44:

Jesus said, Take ye away the stone. Martha, the sister of him that was dead, saith unto him, Lord, by this time he stinketh: for he hath been dead four days. Jesus saith unto her, Said I not unto thee, that, if thou wouldest believe, thou shouldest see the glory of God? Then they took away the stone from the place where the dead was laid. And Jesus lift up his eyes, and said, Father, I thank thee that thou hast heard me. And I knew that thou hearest me always: but because of the people which stand by I said it, that they may believe that thou hast sent me. And when he thus had spoken, he cried with a loud voice, Lazarus, come forth. And he that was dead came forth, bound hand and foot with graveclothes: and his face was bound about with a napkin. Jesus saith unto them, Loose him, and let him go. John 11:39-44

NOTES

Jesus prayed this prayer only for the sake of making deposits. The minds of the onlookers were not renewed, and they needed to come to a place of understanding.

In contrast, there was also a group of people who understood the assignment of declaring and creating but who needed correction. Jesus taught them of the power that was in their mouths, and they now needed to be taught of the spirit in which they were operating…

> **And when his disciples James and John saw this, they said, Lord, wilt thou that we command fire to come down from heaven, and consume them, even as Elias did? But he turned, and rebuked them, and said, Ye know not what manner of spirit ye are of. Luke 9:54-55**

The disciples were fully aware of the power of words; however, they were ready to kill people with this same power. God cannot allow some of us to understand the level of power that we have because we will use it to kill the people.

To Set Order

One of the prophet's assignments is to set order. This assignment overlaps the apostle's assignment. Wherever there is disorder and chaos, the hand of the prophet is required. The establishing of order from chaotic situations requires a prophetic anointing. There are things that cannot be coaxed, loved, or sweet-talked into order.

> **And Jesus went into the temple of God, and cast out all them that sold and bought in the temple, and overthrew the tables of the moneychangers, and the seats of them that sold doves, And said unto them, It is written, My house shall be called the house of prayer; but ye have made it a den of thieves. And the blind and the lame came to him in the temple; and he healed them. Matthew 21:12-14**

We must take notice that, as Jesus restored order in the temple, He did not operate from a sweet-talking, pastoral anointing. He restored order as a prophet.

Before you can set order, you have to be IN order. God may have called you to set order, but until you yourself are in order, you don't have the ability to set order—anywhere.

One of the first obligations of a released prophet is to be a submitted prophet. Our level of submission is a prerequisite to "setting order." Examine your level of support for your man or woman of God. If you don't support him or her, you don't have a right to speak anything into his or her ears. You must be in full support of the one who makes deposits into your life.

Your level of authority comes through the one to whom you are submitted, prophet or not. Listen, God examines and judges your level of authority through your connection and submission to your man or woman of God. God recognizes and deals with you only through the one to whom you are tied. When He looks at your level of authority, He questions it if you are not tied anywhere. When God does look at you, He does so through your man or woman of God.

Unless you are tied and submitted to a man of God, no one will be able to say to you, "You are my son and in you I am well pleased." Take a look at Matthew 3:13-17:

Then cometh Jesus from Galilee to Jordan unto John, to be baptized of him. But John forbad him, saying, I have need to be baptized of thee, and comest thou to me? And Jesus answering said unto him, Suffer it to be so now: for thus it becometh us to fulfill all righteousness. Then he suffered him. And Jesus, when he was baptized, went up straightway out of the water: and, lo, the heavens were opened unto him, and he saw the Spirit of God descending like a dove, and lighting upon him: And lo a voice from heaven, saying, This is my beloved Son, in whom I am well pleased. Matthew 3:13-17

It is important to note that God never announced, "This is my beloved Son, in whom I am well pleased." God's timing is flawless. John the Baptist could not die until he knew that Jesus was the one. Likewise, Jesus didn't fully shine in His ministry until after He bowed and came under the authority of a man's hand. If this was so for Jesus, how much more is it for you and me?

NOTES

Another example of submission is found in the familiar story of Ruth. Naomi had two widowed daughters-in-law whom she strongly admonished to leave her, knowing that she would be unable to bear any more sons for them to wed. To Ruth, this was irrelevant. To Orpah, it was paramount. Ruth clave to Naomi, and Orpah kissed her mother-in-law and left. In conclusion, Ruth married Boaz, the kinsman redeemer and met her destiny head on. Orpah, on the other hand, missed her destiny and needlessly so.

Boaz said to Ruth in the third chapter of the book that bears her name:

And now it is true that I am thy near kinsman: howbeit there is a kinsman nearer than I. Ruth 3:12

Orpah missed her destiny because she didn't want to pay the price of submission. What are you willing to give for your destiny? What are you unwilling to give for your destiny? Refusing to submit to your man or woman of God could very well cost you your destiny.

From this biblical account, it is easy to see how one can miss his or her destiny. The Book of Matthew assists us in understanding how this is indeed possible:

For many are called, but few are chosen. Matthew 22:14

God has indeed called you as a prophet, however, unless a man chooses you, succession is not complete, and ministry is unattainable. If no man chooses you, you remain a "called" prophet with no place or means by which to fulfill your assignment.

Keep in mind, in order to complete your assignment, you must be where God has called you to be and submit in that place. Just any place will not suffice. You must be where God has placed or set you.

And God hath set some in the church, first apostles, secondarily prophets, thirdly teachers, after that miracles, then gifts of healings, helps,

governments, diversities of tongues. 1 Corinthians 12:28

God sets you—you don't make your own choice. God makes the selection, and it is our responsibility to follow up with His selection. When God shifts, you have to shift with Him. When God has set you, you have to "set."

To Prophesy and to Operate in Prophecy

It is the prophet's assignment to not only prophesy but to operate in prophecy. Prophesying alone does not make one a prophet.

It is important to reiterate that not every Christian has the gift of prophecy. In 1 Corinthians 14, we will find that there are several different levels of speaking. They are:

- The gift of tongues
- Unknown tongues (prayer language)
- Divers (different) kinds of tongues
- Other tongues

A lot of denominations teach that not everyone speaks in tongues. Biblically speaking, we find that statement to be false. Every believer has the ability to speak in tongues, but not every believer has the gift of tongues, which is followed by the gift of the interpretation of tongues. As we do a thorough study of 1 Corinthians 14, this information will become a lot clearer.

This is one of the ways by which you can determine that you are in the office of the prophet. These previously mentioned components—in particular, the word of knowledge, the word of wisdom, and discerning of spirits—will frequent your ministry.

Of these components, one that is greatly misquoted and misunderstood is the gift of discerning of spirits. People often make statements such as, "You better watch what you do around me because I have the gift of discernment; I'll discern you!" They are lying! God will not allow anyone to have control over anyone else like that. There are even people who ascribe to this type of teaching and are afraid to go into the presence of a prophet because they think that the prophet will pick up on what they're thinking.

NOTES

Honestly, people are not that sharp. If people can pick up on your thoughts every time you walk into a room, they are very demonic. And not even these demonic people can do that. They're not that sharp, either. Why does the Devil do this? He is the accuser of the brethren, and you are one of the brethren.

God gives us a level of privacy and will not allow it to be invaded, regardless of the anointing upon any prophet. God will not allow your privacy to be invaded unless you refuse to deal with that private area.

For example, you may have sin in your life that you simply will not deal with. In such cases, God may reveal that sin to someone, but only if that someone is confidential. He might reveal it to them not so that you would be exposed in the midst of the congregation, but so that the sin would be exposed *to you* and that you would deal with it. If God decides to do this, it will not be done in a public setting. You will be pulled aside and ministered to appropriately.

God gives you time to deal with your stuff. He won't quickly reveal your stuff, especially to those who will expose it.

Being in the office of the prophet, you will find there are things that are going to frequent your ministry, be evident in your ministry, and be a part of your assignment. They are the word of knowledge, word of wisdom, discerning of spirits, confirmation, revelation, illumination, prophetic utterance, prediction, visions, correction, and ministry confirmation.

Let's talk about correction. Does anyone have the right to just walk up to you and correct you? You better watch it when you correct other people's children.

To Impart Gifts

It is also an assignment of the prophet to impart gifts. As prophets, we must keep in mind that this is to be done with consent. The consent of the individual's man of God is required.

As we discuss this assignment of the prophet, we need to understand three things: there are different kinds of gifts; there are different words and definitions for "gift;" and there are different ways by which these gifts are imparted.

While we embrace what God is saying regarding gifts and re-garding the word "gift," we need to understand that in the King James Version of the Bible there is one spelling of the word "gift." However, in the Greek language there are several different mean-ings for this same word.

When we begin to think about gifts, this question arises: "What is the difference between 'gift' and 'anointing'?" We may mistakenly say that a gifted person is anointed or that an anointed person is gifted. How can we tell the difference?

In the body of Christ, we call a lot of things anointed, and in reality, they are not anointed at all. It was simply a work that was accomplished by someone who was gifted in that area.

One of the ways in which to identify the anointing is found in the Book of Isaiah. When we reach a genuine understanding of what it means to be anointed, we will stop labeling everything as being anointed. We will also learn to observe things prophetically and be able to determine if something or someone is either anointed or gifted.

We can clearly see what qualifies as being anointed in Isaiah 10:27:

> **And it shall come to pass in that day, that his burden shall be taken away from off thy shoul-der, and his yoke from off thy neck, and the yoke shall be destroyed because of the anoint-ing. Isaiah 10:27**

As we zero in on the meaning of the word "anointed," we will grasp what being anointed really means. Experiencing chills that run up and down your spine is not an indication of the anointing. If an individual is really anointed, if the worship service was really anointed, if the choir was really anointed, if the *thing* was really anointed, then burdens were removed and yokes were destroyed.

We must realize that if the speaker excited us and brought about a good effect at the right time, the speaker may not have been anointed as we thought. The speaker may have been gifted.

To receive a clearer understanding, let's imagine the following scenario: We are in a worship service setting. The time has come

NOTES

for the choir to minister in song. Everyone knows that the choir director is really anointed—or is he? Everyone also knows that the choir members are really anointed—or are they? As if on cue, the choir stands and begins to sing with ultimate precision. The director knows exactly when to bring the soprano voices out front and when to shut down all of the other voices. He knows at what point in the song to stop the musicians from playing and have the choir to sing a cappella.

In turn, he knows when to direct the musicians to rejoin the choir voices, causing the choir to reach its maximum potential in vocal performance. As we look around, people are running up and down the aisle, rolling around on the floor, and crying with no end in sight. This was an anointed service! Well, not exactly. Neither the service nor the choir was anointed. No one was set free. No breakthroughs took place. Not one person returned with the testimony that his burdens were removed and his yokes were destroyed. But, they did have a good time. No, the service was not anointed—**but** it was full of gifts.

When we begin to deal with gifts, we must be sure to avoid minimizing them. Everything has its proper place. Gifts are of God. We cannot minimize the gifts and place the anointing on a higher scale. Nor can we minimize the anointing and place the gifts on a higher scale. We must keep them both in proper perspective. When we do this, we will receive an anointing on our gifts. Also, we will find that people will become enlightened and delivered; burdens will be removed and yokes will be destroyed.

The first definition of the English word "gift" that we will discuss is "doma." This is where the word gift—as it pertains to the office—is derived. Whenever we deal with the apostle, prophet, evangelist, pastor, or teacher, the Greek word "doma" applies.

The Greek words "doma" and "charisma," although translated into the same English word "gift," are different from one another. "Doma" classifies you in the office, while "charisma" is a grace gift.

The word "charisma" is defined as a grace gift of which you are not necessarily deserving. This is a gift with which you have been endowed. The definition of this grace gift indicates that its recipient has received an undeserved benefit from God.

88

It must be understood, when discussing the "doma" gift, that if you are going to occupy and execute the office of the apostle or prophet, it is going to be—to some degree—deserved. In addition, once these offices are given or appointed by God, they cannot be given back, nor will God ask that they be returned to Him.

For the gifts and calling of God are without repentance. Romans 11:29

No matter how badly you may want to exchange your office for another one, God won't take it back. Adding to that, even if you desire to occupy your office, you cannot do so until some man recognizes you and pulls you forth into that office.

This is the reason for some of the weird prophets with whom we have come into contact. No one authorized them to walk in their office, yet they do so with no authority or permission. If Jesus had to submit Himself, what makes the prophet exempt from doing so?

As we recall the baptism of Jesus Christ, we realize that He could have never occupied His office had He not bowed under the hand of John the Baptist (Matt. 3). When recalling Jesus' baptism, we are reminded that John did not want to baptize Jesus. In his reluctance, John said to Jesus that he needed to be baptized of Jesus. Well, Jesus never denied that. Instead, Jesus' reply to John was a very interesting one. He said to John in Matthew 3:15, "...*Suffer it to be so now: for thus it becometh us to fulfill all righteousness. Then he suffered him.*"

In other words, Jesus said to John that they needed one another. Jesus could not do what He needed to do without John. Likewise, John could not do what he needed to do without Jesus. Jesus could not have even come forward without His forerunner, John. Besides that, Jesus would have never received the words of approval that His heavenly Father proclaimed upon Him until after He first bowed under John's hand:

And Jesus, when he was baptized, went up straightway out of the water: and, lo, the heavens were opened unto him, and he saw the Spirit of God descending like a dove, and lighting upon him: And lo a voice from heaven, say-

NOTES

ing, **This is my beloved Son, in whom I am well pleased. Matthew 3:16-17**

It cannot be stressed enough that the only way to occupy the office ("doma") is to be willing to bow down to some man. Someone has to announce you, recognize you, and pull you forth into that office.

Has anyone recognized you? Has Jesus even recognized you?

Many will say to me in that day, Lord, Lord, have we not prophesied in thy name? and in thy name have cast out devils? and in thy name done many wonderful works? Matthew 7:22

We must take notice of who asked this question. Some who had cast out devils in His name and had done many marvelous works in His name asked the question. **Unbelievers cannot cast out devils**. Jesus provided us with a witness to this fact in Matthew 12:

And Jesus knew their thoughts, and said unto them, Every kingdom divided against itself is brought to desolation; and every city or house divided against itself shall not stand: And if Satan cast out Satan, he is divided against himself; how shall then his kingdom stand? Matthew 12:25-26

Considering the marvelous works that these persons had done, how could Jesus declare that He never knew them? In short, He said that He wouldn't even recognize them. This brings us back to the place of succession. The only way that God recognizes us is by and through who links us to Him. There must be someone who links us to God. We are not "IT." This fact may be a tough pill to swallow, but it is a prescription worth taking.

We must realize that if we make a decision, based upon our feelings, to become part of something that God has never authorized us to become a part of, then we are out of place. As long as we remain out of place, God will recognize only the things that we have done prior to the point that we removed ourselves from the place where He assigned us to be. Regardless of the great works that we accomplished, if we are not where God told us to be, nothing that we do will be recognized.

Be mindful, however, that God will not always tell you to go. There will be times when you will have to know that it is the will of God for you in order to shift because you know the will and purpose of God for your life. If God is going to recognize a work, you will find His signature of approval at the bottom of the page.

Following the discussion of "doma," we arrive at the gift "charisma." This gift, as we mentioned earlier, differs from the "doma" gift. From your mother's womb, God assigned you to a particular office. Once you've gone through the process and submitted yourself to a man, there will be particular ways that the "charisma" gift can come upon you. Those ways are as follows:

Methods of Impartation

1. Gift by Relationship—2 Timothy 1:3-6

This is an endowed gift by biological relationship. This gift is on Timothy for no reason other than it traveled down through his bloodline.

This is also true for some of us. The only reason that we operate in a particular gift is because of some of our biological fathers and mothers. This explains why particular gifts were on you, even as a child. This is why you dreamed the dreams you dreamt. Tragically, we never received the proper training required to nurture these gifts.

2. Gift by Fellowship or Oil—1 Timothy 4:13-14

As we consider this passage of scripture, we could also call this gift a "**gift by permission**." Paul said in the thirteenth verse, "*Till I come…*" indicating that there is a time period allotted to Timothy. In addition, we come to know that Timothy has not been left alone. The presbytery is present with him to both oversee him and to participate with Paul in releasing the gifts.

We know from the scriptures that Paul recognized Timothy as his son. Knowing this, we are aware that whatever was on Paul would come upon Timothy. But, a release had to take place in

NOTES

order for Timothy to actually receive and walk in the same things that the apostle Paul walked in. What we must keep foremost in mind as we discuss this gift is that outside of fellowship, Timothy would have never received this gift.

Some of us want particular things to come upon us but refuse to hook in. If we don't hook in, they will never happen. Maintaining a long-distance relationship will not do the trick. A level of fellowship and commitment has to take place. There are times when we make the decision to not draw near or come close in a relationship. Yet, we declare that we want what's on the man or woman of God. How badly do you really want it?

The mother of James and John made a request of Jesus for her sons. Jesus responded with a question for her sons. He asked them in Matthew 20:22, "*Are ye able to drink of the cup that I shall drink of, and to be baptized with the baptism that I am baptized with?*" In simpler terms, He asked them if they were able to walk closely with Him. How about you?

Are you able to walk closely with your man or woman of God? It is the level of closeness in which you walk in fellowship with them that will determine the measure of the gift to be imparted. Sadly enough, some will not be able to receive the gift because they cannot handle walking that closely with their man or woman of God. A prime example of this is found in Acts 13:2.

As they ministered to the Lord, and fasted, the Holy Ghost said, Separate me Barnabas and Saul for the work whereunto I have called them. Acts 13:2

In this biblical account we see that Saul and Barnabas were being separated as apostles. Prior to this separation, there was someone who used to hang with Paul at a particular level, but was not able to handle what was on Paul. His name was John Mark. Consequently, John Mark journeyed on with Barnabas, and Paul was accompanied by another young man who was able to walk with him—someone who, shortly afterwards, ended up in prison with Paul. His name was Silas. Silas was both willing AND able to walk with Paul. As a result of Silas' endurance, what was on Paul came on him.

Are you able to actually do what your man or woman of God does? Jesus only asked James and John about their ability to drink of the cup that He would drink from, and to be baptized with the baptism that He would be baptized with, so that they might have an understanding of their potential. In you is the potential to do what your man or woman of God does. The deciding factor is your willingness to pay the price to do it.

Can you really handle walking so closely with your man or woman of God? You must be completely honest in your answer. Do not walk with your leader and then take your hands from the plow and run away. The next time you want to follow, the leader may not grant you permission to do so.

3. Gift by Transfer—Romans 1:11

You cannot even be established without the gift by transfer.

YOUR GIFT WILL OBLIGATE YOU AND CAUSE YOU TROUBLE.

Paul is conscious, as we discuss the gift by transfer, not to lay hands on the people to transfer the gifts too quickly. When the gift is transferred, you're asking for trouble. Many people have been jumping in everyone's line and now find themselves wondering where all of their troubles have come from. What has actually happened is that they've jumped in someone's line and something was transferred. Stop jumping.

The Bible tells us not to lay hands on any man suddenly. Why? Because when someone lays their hands upon you, they're causing trouble for you. Yet, this gift can only come by way of transfer.

The apostle Paul, in the Book of Romans, proclaims how he longed to see the people to whom he might impart some spiritual gift. Paul was the carrier of something. The minute that Paul laid his hands on them with purpose in mind, the gifts that were on Paul transferred to them.

4. Gift by Proximity—1 Samuel 10:5-6

Let's recap this story. In this account, the gift is not actually on

NOTES

93

Saul. Saul meets a company of prophets who have just finished worshipping and will prophesy. This company of prophets will prophesy. But as these prophets get closer and closer to Saul, and as Saul gets closer and closer to them, what's on the prophets will come onto Saul. Saul, in turn, will do what the prophets do and prophesy.

As long as Saul was in the proximity of the prophets, he was able to do as they do and prophesy. Once Saul and the prophets were no longer in proximity of one another, the gift that came on Saul to prophesy *with* the prophets would cease to be upon Saul. He could only operate in this gift as long as he was in the atmosphere of the gift.

We see this taking place in our present day. People may enter the atmosphere of the prophetic, even though they are not prophetic, and do what prophets do. This is possible merely because of the presence of the anointing.

For example, when there is a weighty anointing on you, once your gift has been used and someone takes the platform immediately after you have left, there is an anointing and a gifting that remains. Therefore, whoever takes the platform may operate in that anointing and gifting simply because he or she came into the proximity of that gift. But, if that same person attempts to operate in that gift after moving from the proximity of that gift, the person will fail. The gift was imparted by proximity. It was a borrowed anointing.

It is paramount that we understand how gifts are imparted. Once we understand this, we will have to take close notice of how we are to impart these gifts, provided that we are at the level needed to do so.

In addition, prior to imparting gifts, you must take close inventory of the person you will lay hands upon to impart gifts or the anointing, lest you anoint something that God hates. If you anoint a rebel, that rebel becomes an anointed rebel. We have to examine what needs to be examined before we lay hands on people. Take stock of what a person is. If you fail to do so and lay hands on the person anyway, you could cause a great deal of trouble.

To Speak to the Hearts of Kings

> **Then the king of Syria warred against Israel, and took counsel with his servants, saying, In such and such a place shall be my camp. And the man of God sent unto the king of Israel, saying, Beware that thou pass not such a place; for thither the Syrians are come down. And the king of Israel sent to the place which the man of God told him and warned him of, and saved himself there, not once nor twice. Therefore the heart of the king of Syria was sore troubled for this thing; and he called his servants, and said unto them, Will ye not shew me which of us is for the king of Israel? And one of his servants said, None, my lord, O king: but Elisha, the prophet that is in Israel, telleth the king of Israel the words that thou speakest in thy bedchamber. 2 Kings 6:8-12**

It is important to remember that "kings" may refer to royalty, presidents, government officials, or persons in high places of authority.

This assignment is very important to understand. We will find that there are some persons who may perform this assignment who fall into the category of seers.

Seers should not try to prophesy. They should only make the attempt to release information into the ear of the king. A seer sees downward into a particular, concentrated area. The seer knows where to bomb the area. He knows how to make intercession regarding a particular area that will annihilate the works of the Enemy.

If the seer doesn't see outside of the concentrated area, when he tries to prophesy, he will not be able to see the ambush that has been set farther down the road. Essentially, seers are unable to speak to anything outside of their concentrated area. If they *do* prophesy to an individual, the recipient of that word will end up being defeated. His defeat will come because the seer (who tried to prophesy) failed to see what lied ahead. He may have seen what this person would come into and where they were at the time; however, the seer didn't see the rest of the picture.

NOTES

95

If you are operating as a seer, your assignment is to speak into the king's ear so that the king will understand what's happening on the battleground. Don't send the king to the battlefield unprepared.

The seers are considered "bombers." This is why it is important that seers are confidential people who are not trying to prophesy something. If the seer attempts to prophesy, he may end up speaking the very information the Enemy wants to know in order to lay the next trap. Oftentimes, when we are going to bomb something, we don't need to verbalize it. We just need to bomb it.

If you see a trap laid for your man or woman of God, it is not time to talk about it. Bomb it! Bomb it and be quiet about it! No one is impressed by your ability to see into the realm of the spirit. By talking about what you see, you are only giving the Devil information that he doesn't even have.

The Devil has information that he wouldn't have if the body of Christ hadn't given it to him. The Devil doesn't understand seasons and times; nor does he have hearing access into the realm of the spirit. He can't even break the code on your tongues. So, any information he gets is because you verbalize the information in a language that he has learned.

How does the Devil acquire information in order to communicate that same information to a demon? How does the Devil acquire information in order to communicate that same information to a palm reader? Some Christian picked it up in the realm of the spirit and verbalized it when it shouldn't have been verbalized.

If there is something that needs to be bombed, bomb it! But, if God just wants to share information with you as a result of His fellowship with you, keep it!

There will be times, because of His relationship with you, God will just want to fellowship with you. In those times, He may share information with you. God actually had this kind of relationship with Adam. In the third chapter of Genesis, we can even find God **looking** for Adam: "*And they heard the voice of the Lord God walking in the garden in the cool of the day: and Adam and his wife hid themselves from the presence of the Lord God amongst the trees of the garden. And the Lord God called*

*unto Adam, and said unto him, **Where art thou***?" (Gen. 3:8-9)
When God wants to talk with someone, does He need to look
for someone else because He knows that you will release the
information He shared with you before it's time to release it?

To Establish Churches, Ministries, Businesses, and Training Facilities

The prophet has been given a unique ability. He has been
gifted to see into a person's life and to determine his or her passions. With this information, the prophet will be able to assist
and guide this person to a place where he or she can turn these
passions into businesses and ministries.

As prophets, we thought that the bulk of our responsibility
was to prophesy. There is so much more to being a prophet than
prophesying. How many churches have you established? How
many ministries? What about businesses and training facilities?
What have you done outside of prophesying?

Prophets understand seasons and times. We know that the
sons of Issachar had understanding of times and knew what Israel ought to do (1 Chron. 12:32). If this is true, and it is, then
as prophets we should be able to tell people what they ought to
do. Again, if given the right information, we should be able to
talk with someone and, shortly thereafter, tell him or her what he
or she ought to do.

Each and every one of us has a business on the inside of us. If
we would quit being such chickens, we would eventually be able
to stop going on our nine-to-five jobs to make someone else
rich.

That something on the inside of us (the niche) will make us
rich. What is on the inside of you that you have not pursued? What
is it that God has placed there? We will discuss this in further detail as we examine the marketplace prophet.

This same unique ability will enable the prophet to give wise
counsel as it pertains to governing and establishing churches and
training facilities.

Like the apostle, the prophet is a special messenger from God.
The prophet is the one divinely inspired to communicate God's

NOTES

will to His people and to disclose the future to them. The primary reason or purpose for the prophet is that of declaring, announcing, or uttering a communication from God to man.

The prophet has a practical office to discharge. His essential purpose is to be an "interpreter" for God. Within the prophet's commission is to show the people of God their transgressions and sins. It is the prophet's duty to admonish and reprove, to denounce prevailing sins, to warn the people with the terrors of divine judgment, and to call them to repentance. As well, the prophet brings the message of consolation and pardon.

Prophets may also maintain the role of pastors or ministerial monitors of the people. Prophets could have the responsibility of one or more ascension gift. But the apostle, pastor, evangelist, or teacher may or may not be prophetic. One may be in one office, yet flow in an anointing from another office.

In the Old Testament, the prophet's function differed from that of the New Testament church leader or priest. The priest approached God on behalf of men by means of sacrifice. The prophet comes to men as an ambassador from God, appealing to them to turn from their evil ways and lives. The person maintaining the office of the prophet has the authority to rebuke the leadership offices of the church, providing that they are released as prophets. Those functioning within the boundaries of prophetic ministry have the responsibility to encourage and not to rebuke.

The prophetic and priestly classes were not antagonistic, or in opposition to one another. The prophet was to understand all aspects of the church and God's plans and expectations of the full church body. This is extremely necessary if or when church leadership (the priesthood) gets out of the will of God. The one in the office the prophet is raised to give severe rebuke.

In the Old Testament, the prophet's role in relationship to government was in exerting godly influence upon rulers and state affairs. The prophet was not an officer of the state, but a special messenger from God.

CHAPTER 9—Chapter Review

1. Describe each of the prophet's assignments as discussed in this chapter.

2. Define gossip and how will it hinder you from fulfilling your prophetic assignment.

3. What are two major components of the prophet's assignment?

4. Describe the different levels of speaking as found in 1 Corinthians 14.

5. Discuss the Greek translations for the word "gift" and how each translation differs from the other in function and in operation.

6. Describe the methods of impartation identified in this chapter.

NOTES
CHAPTER 10—The New Testament Prophet

The ministry of the New Testament prophet is submitted and responsible to the ministry of the apostle. The prophetic ministry is a valid ascension gift ministry given to the church by Jesus. The prophetic office is under (and accountable) to the apostolic office. This is because all functioning of the prophetic office must be based upon the historical facts and teachings of Jesus Christ, as was recorded by the apostles.

The prophet must understand his or her purpose in order to be an effectual prophet. So, in order to be effectual, one must understand the purpose of the prophet.

Like the apostle, the prophet is a special messenger from God. The prophet is the one divinely inspired to communicate God's will to His people and to disclose the future to them. The primary purpose for the prophet is declaring, announcing, or uttering a communication from God to man.

The prophet has a practical office to discharge. His essential purpose is to be an "interpreter" for God. Within the prophet's commission is to show the people of God their transgressions and sins, to admonish and reprove, to denounce prevailing sins, to warn the people with the terrors of divine judgment, and to call them to repentance. As well, the prophet brings the message of consolation and pardon.

Prophets may also maintain the role of pastors and/or ministerial monitors of the people. They could have the responsibility of one or more ascension gift. But the apostle, pastor, evangelist, or teacher may or may not be prophetic. One may be in one office, yet flow in an anointing from another office, but nobody holds two offices.

In the Old Testament, the prophet's function differed from that of the New Testament church leader or priest. The priest approached God on behalf of men by means of sacrifice. The prophet comes to men as an ambassador from God, appealing to them to turn from their evil ways and life. This person maintaining the office of the prophet has the authority to rebuke the leadership offices of the church, providing that the person is released as a prophet. Those functioning within the boundaries of prophetic ministry have the responsibility to encourage and not to rebuke.

The prophetic and priestly classes were not antagonistic, or in opposition to another. The prophet was to understand all aspects of the church and God's plans and expectations of the full church body. This is extremely necessary if or when church leadership (the priesthood) moves out of the will of God. The one in the office of the prophet is raised to give severe rebuke. However, it is mandatory that the prophet move in absolute wisdom.

In the Old Testament, the prophet's role in relationship to government was in exerting godly influence upon rulers and state affairs. The prophet was not an officer of the state, but a special messenger from God.

To Become a Voice of God

In Matthew 3:1-3, the Word said that John was a voice crying in the wilderness, "…prepare ye the way of the Lord, make his paths straight." John was a powerful vehicle (or prophet) that God chose to use. Through John, God caused the Word of His Son to continue to go forth as the final proclamation of the coming of Jesus Christ. God uses the prophet to bring about change to educate in order to reproduce. This is one of the ways in which God speaks audibly. He speaks in your inner ear, by dreams and by visions, yet all should be a confirmation of what God has already said.

To Receive Prophetic Responsibility

Old Testament prophets were categorized as "seers." They had a great responsibility to the kings and leaders who depended upon them to both see and hear accurately. God placed the responsibility of the nations on the prophets. For that reason, the sons of Issachar had understanding of times and knew what Israel ought to do (1 Chron. 12:32).

> **And he said unto him, Behold now, there is in this city a man of God, and he is an honourable man; all that he saith cometh surely to pass:**

NOTES

101

_____
_____
_____
_____
_____
_____
_____
_____
_____
_____
_____
_____
_____
_____
_____
_____

now let us go thither; peradventure he can shew us our way that we should go. 1 Samuel 9:6

To Illustrate Accountability

Many times, in the midst of being lost, God will speak to the prophet. The prophet must maintain accountability. To whom are you accountable? It is **mandatory** that the prophet maintain a line of open communication with the Lord, his covering, a good relationship with people, and integrity in the sight of the recipient of the Word. The lack of accountability and integrity destroys the charge one may have for a greater anointing.

To Usher In Change

Whenever God decides to bring about change, He always calls for a prophet. God ushered in change during the period of time when the Jews had begun to relax in their spirit. They became very religious. God sent the prophet, John the Baptist, **as a voice** to prepare the way. This was because it was the appointed time for Jesus to enter the earth. The purpose of the prophet that must be remembered is that he promotes the vision of another and introduces the visionary. Therefore, the prophet has a word regarding what God is doing.

Often, when this voice sounds, there is no "Thus saith the Lord" to signal to you that it is God.

Surely the Lord God will do nothing, but he revealeth his secret unto his servants the prophets. Amos 3:7

The prophet prepares the way for a new move or another move of God. John the Baptist introduced Jesus, which was a new move (Matt. 3:11).

There is a great need to develop the voice of the prophetic utterance in today's church. A person may be receiving and speaking a one-word prophecy and have to graduate to paragraphs of utterances. God never limits us to one word, but does expect us to develop our prophetic vocabulary and sensitivity to that which He is saying. This brings us to the making of the prophet and prophetic people. If you are to be a prophetic voice, you will go through the making.

Prophetic utterance should bring forth prophetic truth. As a prophetic voice, deliverance should come forth from the prophet.

Ephesians 4:11 identifies the role of the church leadership that Jesus Christ ordained for the plan and operation of the New Testament church. Our focus is on the purpose for which God gave these prophets and how they correlate with the four other offices within the church.

NOTES

CHAPTER 10—Chapter Review

1. How does the New Testament prophet differ from the Old Testament prophet?

2. What are some of the ways in which God will speak?

3. What are the four primary areas of focus for the prophet?

CHAPTER 11—The Development of the Prophet

The Undeveloped, Underdeveloped, and Developed Prophet

In case you haven't noticed yet, God places pressure on you to provoke you to produce at your maximum—even when you don't know what your maximum is. For this reason, prophets go through tremendous trials because God has to press out of them the oil that they never knew existed inside of them. There are particular levels of the prophet and of the prophet type that must "ooze" out of your pores. The only way this will take place is if God places a level of pressure upon you and allows you to go through things that will begin to develop you in particular areas.

As we discuss the undeveloped, underdeveloped, and developed prophet, we will find that we have existed for far too long in the place of the undeveloped or underdeveloped prophet. In fact, most people within the body of Christ—to some degree—have made it all right for us to operate as undeveloped or underdeveloped prophets and yet live as if we were developed prophets. We have now reached a point, however, where God is placing pressure on us to cease from operating as undeveloped and underdeveloped prophets. We must now be willing to receive the instruction and training that will cause us to operate at our maximum and to become the developed prophet whom God desires.

The **undeveloped prophet** is a prophet who has not been developed to any level or degree. The **underdeveloped prophet** is a prophet who has been partially developed and has experienced just enough growth to fool some folks. And last, the **developed prophet** is a prophet who has withstood training, tests, trials, and temptations and, as a result, has been released into the prophetic office. This prophet is ready for "frontline" battle.

Why do most of us exist as undeveloped or underdeveloped prophets? The answer may surprise you. Most of us exist as undeveloped or underdeveloped prophets because we refuse to be hidden.

Even though you may have some clue that you're a prophet, God still wants to hide you. He doesn't want you to put "prophet" on your business cards or to place your "prophet" plaque on the outside of your office door. He doesn't want you to tell anyone. For the sake of understanding your purpose and direction for your life, He wants you to know who you are, but He doesn't want you to reveal your identity to anyone. He wants to hide you so that He can work on you. You must welcome this fact while He develops you.

If we look at the life of Jesus, we find a powerful principle that teaches the importance of remaining hidden. There was a particular period in Jesus' life when people would stumble upon who Jesus was, and He would direct them not to tell anyone. What would they do? They would go and tell it. Anytime they told someone who Jesus was, He had to leave the city. Jesus had to make sure that He remained hidden until His time to be revealed came. I wish somebody had told me, "Rodney, just stay in hiding until God gets done with you."

When you get to the place where you are in hiding, and you know that you're in hiding, it is then that God is able to work on you without interruption. It doesn't take as long at this point. The reason most of us are either undeveloped or underdeveloped is that whenever God is able to get us to a position where He can work on us and where He can put pressure on us, we move. In other words, we try to tell someone who we are. They, in turn, try to pull on us, and we end up being pulled out of position. The objective is to stay in hiding long enough for God to work on us.

When we are in hiding, God works on us in various ways. Three of the things that God deals with concerning prophets in hiding are pride, the "if you are" test, and the submission test.

Pride. Every prophet, at one point or another in his or her growth, will deal with the spirit of pride. It is a battle that cannot be avoided. Before prophets are developed, they must learn to recognize and defeat this spirit, lest it wreak havoc in their ministry and their lives.

The "if you are" test. Most of the time, we battle and fail this test. This test places prophets in the position where they must prove that they are really prophets. If we had remained in hiding, there would have been no need for this particular test. No one would have known that you called yourself a prophet. Therefore, the opportunity to challenge you to prove yourself as such would never have presented itself.

Submission. Most prophets fail this test several times before passing. You have to be sharp for the test of submission, so sharp that your mission gets lost in that leader's mission. It is imperative that you arrive at the point in your life where even though you realize that you have a ministry, you actually declare, like Jesus, "My will is to do the will of him who sent me." Then you have to figure out who sent you. Did God send you, or did your man or woman of God send you? Who sent you?

The Bible tells us that many are called but few are chosen (Matt. 20:16). The one who chooses you is actually the one who sends you. One of the things we have to understand is that God calls you. No one else can call you. God is the only one who can call you, but He leaves it up to man to choose you. Unless we come to the point where we have been selected and chosen, hand-picked by man, we have no right to ministry.

Let's take a look at Joshua 1:1, which reads,

> **Now after the death of Moses the servant of the Lord it came to pass, that the Lord spake unto Joshua the son of Nun, Moses' minister, saying, Joshua 1:1**

Wasn't Joshua God's minister? Well then, who was Moses? God's servant? Joshua was, as a matter of fact, Moses' minister, and Moses was the servant of the Lord. Understand that if I am the leader and you are sent to me, we both can't be the servants of God. God is going to give direction to the one who is called, hand-picked, and anointed to serve Him.

If we go a little further into the Book of Numbers, we find God talking to Moses:

> **And the Lord said unto Moses, Gather unto me seventy men of the elders of Israel, whom thou knowest to be the elders of the people, and officers over them; and bring them unto the tabernacle of the congregation, that they may stand there with thee. And I will come down and talk with thee there: and I will take of the spirit which is upon thee, and will put it upon them; and they shall bear the burden of the people**

NOTES

with thee, that thou bear it not thyself alone.
Numbers 11:16-17

Please notice that God took of **the spirit that was upon Moses** and placed it upon the seventy who were elders indeed. "Moses, if you have some trouble out of them, it's your own fault because you selected them, you chose them, and then you sent them to do what I called you to do."

You have to know where you're assigned and to whom you're assigned. Just because you don't like the church doesn't mean you can jump up and leave. First Corinthians 12:28 lets us know, *"And God hath set some in the church, first apostles, secondarily prophets, thirdly teachers, after that miracles, then gifts of healings, helps, governments, diversities of tongues."* Who set them in the church? God.

If you are at a particular church and God leads you, you must have been sent and set by God. If you are potted in that place as a flower is potted by God, no one should "repot" you except God. There's no "repotting" done except when the gardener, God, "repots" you. Any flower that can plant and "repot" itself is a freak of nature and of no use in the Kingdom. God will send you to a place so that you can be made, not so that you can uproot and "repot" yourself whenever you encounter something that doesn't tickle your fancy.

Wherever God sets you, you must stay put because you're going through a serious test of submission. I know, "They talk to me like a dog! They talk to me like I'm stupid or something! Submit? I ain't submitting to nothin'!" Well, you just failed the test.

Submission—Case in Point: Mark 7:24-29—The Syrophenician Woman

The Syrophenician woman went to Jesus and besought Him that He would cast the Devil out of her child. Jesus responded, *"Let the children first be filled: for it is not meet to take the children's bread, and to cast it unto the dogs."* She began her response with the following words, *"Yes Lord: yet..."* How did she address Him? She called Him "Lord" after being recognized as a dog. In essence, what she said was, "Jesus, it doesn't matter to me if I pick it up off the floor or if it's leftovers. The only thing I want is for my request to be answered." In turn, Jesus complimented her on her faith. That's all she needed to hear Him say— "You got what you asked for." Her request was filled only because she passed the submission test.

As a prophet, passing the submission test is a must. If the spirit of pride had been present in this Syropheonician woman, she would have risen up at being compared to a dog. But, she didn't. She passed the pride test. In like manner, should your man or woman of God say something that you don't like, you need to lie down like a dog, roll over, and play dead.

The developed prophet has mastered this response. The undeveloped and underdeveloped prophet have yet to move into this place of maturity and humility where the spirit of pride is ruled over and not a ruler. In this hour, we as prophets must endeavor to become developed so that the prophetic voice can be released in the earth, so that God's will, mind, and purposes might be made known.

The Budding Prophet

Many of you may already have an idea of where you fit in the prophetic, while others may still be discovering their particular place within this ministry or office. Regardless of your specific assignment, you must have identified by now if you are an undeveloped, underdeveloped, or developed prophet. Now, however, we've arrived at the **budding prophct**. In this portion of the book, we will learn what a budding prophet is and what his assignment entails.

The budding prophet is a prophet who has been hand-picked for development. This prophet type has not yet reached the full stage of development, but he or she is "knee-deep" in the development process.

One of the best examples of a budding prophet lies in the story of Elijah and Elisha. When we trail the life of Elisha, we will learn that Elisha was found walking behind oxen and not in a tent passing out his business cards. He was called as a prophet, but he was not fulfilling any portion of the prophetic. As a budding prophet, it is important to know where you fit within the scope of the prophetic.

NOTES

As we deal with 1 Kings 19, we will explore the situation that surrounded Elijah's life and what Elisha was walking into. This is the part of the prophetic that we don't understand. You see, when you hooked up with your man or woman of God, you were walking into something. Whether or not you understood what was actually taking place is irrelevant; the fact remained that you indeed walked into something when you made the connection. God, on the other hand, understood everything. He knew exactly what you were walking into and knew that what you were walking into would be for your development.

Most of us are familiar with the life of Elijah and with both his victories and defeats. We love to recall his victories, but we must realize that amongst his many successes, Elijah had particular issues. If we revisit his life, we will remember that one of his issues came with the name "Jezebel" written on it. Jezebel had it out for Elijah. Elijah, at this juncture in his life, had encountered victory on the mount where he literally called down fire. He called down fire and then ran from a woman called Jezebel. Anytime prophets meet up with trouble, they run into their caves.

In 1 Kings 19:9, the Bible tells us,

And he came thither unto a cave, and lodged there; and, behold, the word of the Lord came to him, and he said unto him, What doest thou here, Elijah? 1 Kings 19:9

Elijah, in a time of trouble, ran to a cave and lodged there. He wasn't even thinking about coming out of that cave. But, the Bible says that the Word of the Lord came to him even when he was in the cave. You must understand that whenever purpose is on you and in you, the Word of the Lord will find you, regardless of where you run.

When you run to your respective caves, don't expect to get another Word from God. Once in your cave, will you receive the Word that comes to you? Listen. You will get the same Word in your cave that Elijah received: "What are you doing here?"

After all that you've gone through, after all of the things that God delivered you from, after receiving forgiveness for the things you've done, after surviving all of the things that people did to you, what could you possibly be doing in the cave? God

110

just doesn't understand. God looks at the deposit that He placed inside of you, and for that reason He doesn't understand why you're in the cave. He realizes that the deposit within you is greater than the situations that surround you.

I understand that oftentimes we try to get away so that we can hear God. But, how many times do we have to run away to hear Him?

God needs a prophet who can go through the battle and still hear Him. He needs us to be able to be in the midst of a storm and to say, "Peace be still" and still be able to hear Him. Then, the storm can resume.

Be aware of the fact that you are in control of the stuff around you—the stuff around you is not in control of you. You cannot, however, tell the stuff around you to be still because it has a purpose. It has to fulfill its course, but it must not be permitted to interrupt what God is saying to you.

Understand: *A sabbatical is not undertaken so that you can hear God. A sabbatical is intended for you to get yourself together*.

In 1 Kings 19:10, Elijah declares his jealousy for the Lord.

> **And he said, I have been very jealous for the Lord God of hosts: for the children of Israel have forsaken thy covenant, thrown down thine altars, and slain thy prophets with the sword; and I, even I only, am left; and they seek my life, to take it away. 1 Kings 19:10**

In other words, Elijah said, "I'm jealous. They forsook your covenant and threw down your altars, and have slain your prophets with the sword, and I'm the only one that's left who's been doing it right. I can't figure out, God, why you won't do something about this woman who is after me and is seeking to take my life!" As prophets, a lot of times we feel as if we're doing something that no one else is doing, and we can't figure out why we were dealt such a bitter hand.

In the following verses, 1 Kings 19:11-12, God told Elijah to leave the cave:

NOTES

111

And he said, Go forth, and stand upon the mount before the Lord. And, behold, the Lord passed by, and a great and strong wind rent the mountains, and brake in pieces the rocks before the Lord; but the Lord was not in the wind: and after the wind an earthquake; but the Lord was not in the earthquake: And after the earthquake a fire; but the Lord was not in the fire: and after the fire a still small voice. 1 Kings 19:11-12

Remember that Elijah went *running* into the cave. What does your cave look like? Let's not just think of the cave as some place that we retreat to from life's storms. When you didn't want anything else to do with another man, you retreated to a cave. What cave? The cave of "no-man." You retreated to a place where you would never encounter another man. The same holds true for the man who wanted nothing else to do with a woman. When you became fed up with or hurt by leadership, you retreated to a cave. What cave? The cave of "leaders with no leadership ability." Many times when we are in this situation, we will search out and connect with a leader who really has no leadership ability to avoid the potential of being hurt again. Retreating is not the answer. As God told Elijah, I must tell you, "Go forth and stand."

The command to go forth and stand is very important to the life of the budding prophet. Before God allowed the wind to come, He told Elijah to do two things: Go forth and stand. The budding prophet has to be willing to be taught how to do these two things.

As we considered 1 Kings 19:11-12, we saw that God was not in the earthquake, the great wind, or the fire. He was in the still, small voice. We should never be led by the results of the great wind, earthquake, or fire. Often we refuse to go forth and stand because our focus is placed on the earthquake, the wind, or the fire instead of on going forth and standing. If you are going to effectively bud as a prophet, you are going to have to have someone in your life who knows how to walk through a tragedy without being shaken from purpose.

Let's take a look at 1 Kings 19:14-19:

And he said, I have been very jealous for the Lord God of hosts: because the children of Israel have forsaken thy covenant, thrown

down thine altars, and slain thy prophets with the sword; and I, even I only, am left; and they seek my life, to take it away. And the Lord said unto him, Go, return on thy way to the wilderness of Damascus: and when thou comest, anoint Hazael to be king over Syria: And Jehu the son of Nimshi shalt thou anoint to be king over Israel: and Elisha the son of Shaphat of Abel-meholah shalt thou anoint to be prophet in thy room. And it shall come to pass, that him that escapeth the sword of Hazael shall Jehu slay: and him that escapeth from the sword of Jehu shall Elisha slay. Yet I have left me seven thousand in Israel, all the knees which have not bowed unto Baal, and every mouth which hath not kissed him. So he departed thence, and found Elisha the son of Shaphat, who was plowing with twelve yoke of oxen before him, and he with twelfth: and Elijah passed by him, and cast his mantle upon him. 1 Kings 19:14-19

In verse 14, the "I" syndrome makes an appearance. Notice how many times Elijah uses the word "I." His use of this word is a clear indication that he is still concerned that the folks did not measure up to how he was walking.

In verse 15, God tells Elijah to return to the wilderness, but this time his return to the wilderness will bring him into contact with someone. This time his trip through the wilderness is to anoint someone. And last but not least, "Elijah, why don't we just go ahead and replace you. Elijah, I realize that you're stressed out, but you are coming very close to becoming self-righteous, yet, you still have your mind on Me. Because of your purpose, Elijah, I can't allow you to become this self-righteous man. I must get you out of this. I must replace you before you become this person. Yes, you are anointed, but I cannot permit self-righteousness to dwell and mature in you."

Now enters Elisha. What in the world could Elisha possibly gain from a man like Elijah? What could he possibly want from such a man? Why would he want to follow a man who had so many issues? To Elisha, none of these things mattered. He was ready to bud as a prophet and willing to do what it took to get himself there. He wasn't interested in how Elijah failed but in how he overcame his failures.

In verse 19, we see that the mantle was shifted. Elijah had to have a successor. At this point, he was more conscious of succession than he was of selfishness. He understood that Elisha was who he was since God had already preordained him to be the prophet in his room or to be his successor. When a successor is selected, the demon of jealousy raises its ugly head.

We learned that there were seven thousand who had not bowed the knee to or kissed Baal, yet Elisha was chosen as the successor. God picked a boy who was walking behind oxen and who was loyal to his biological father and overlooked the seven thousand previously mentioned. That's enough to provoke jealousy in anyone's heart! As a matter of fact, many of us would have been offended by this selection. But, how could we have been? We didn't know that person's story.

What exactly is Elisha's story? Well, he was plowing behind twelve oxen and tending to his father's business. HE WAS WORKING. God provides for people who are working. Do you realize how many people want to be married? They will uproot all of the men or women who are hanging out and will attend the church that has the most available men or women. They become watchers and never really get anyone. If God is to present them, they must work. Likewise, if you're looking for the anointing to descend upon you, stop looking. God will not place the anointing on you simply because you're chasing it. He will place the anointing upon you when you become very conscious of your man or woman of God's assignment and less conscious of your own assignment. Most of us, however, are still chasing the anointing and have yet to apprehend it.

Elisha didn't chase the anointing or the mantle. It was cast upon him. This investiture, in simple terms, said, "Follow me." You can't just cast your anointed mantle upon just anyone. You have to make sure that people have "staying power." I am not passing my mantle on to just anybody. I can't do it. You can't do it. You can't just tell anyone to follow you. And, you can't beg anyone to follow you, either. Elijah said it one time only, and he didn't actually *say* it. Elisha, however, knew exactly what the casting of the mantle meant. He knew that he was budding and made the proper arrangements to follow Elijah.

Elisha's response to receiving Elijah's mantle shows his deep sense of loyalty. The boy had himself together! Elisha agreed to follow Elijah but first bid his parents goodbye. He requested that he be allowed to go and kiss his father and mother, and after doing so, left that assignment to follow Elijah. He acknowledged the shifting of the mantle and his own willingness to follow Elijah, but managed to stay in order and obtain a release from his parents first.

In addition, prior to leaving his parents, Elisha offered a sacrifice. He was in order. He was ready to bud as a prophet. How many of you feel that you are ready to bud as a prophet? Well, what does your tithing record look like? Do you even tithe? What about sacrificial giving?

After Elisha made the proper arrangements, he arose and went after Elijah to serve and minister to him. He became Elijah's minister. The Bible didn't acknowledge him as a minister of God, but as Elijah's minister; Elisha served a man. This serving prepared him for budding. Until budding prophets learn that they must serve the person to whom they are submitted, they will always remain in a stage of "undevelopment" or "underdevelopment."

In 2 Kings 2, we observe how Elisha endured everything that his man of God, Elijah, endured. His perseverance entitled him to the anointing that was on the prophet Elijah and to the anointing that Elijah stood in line to receive. "What if my man of God does not live out his full course?" If you serve your man of God and he leaves this life early, you are entitled to the anointing that was on him at the time of his departure and to the anointing that never came to him.

Your heart of service toward the man of God determines the level of anointing that you are actually entitled to. Please notice the definite article "**the**." Someone is responsible for making sure that the correct endowment comes upon you. Someone is responsible for hearing God in what He says regarding you. It is of the utmost importance that you know you are set and carved out in a place intricately designed for you. That place is found as you submit to your man or woman of God. Budding prophets, if they are to effectively bud into developed prophets, must realize this and seek to submit themselves so that they might be what they were created to be.

NOTES

CHAPTER 11—Chapter Review

1. What does it mean to be undeveloped, underdeveloped, or developed as a prophet? Indicate behaviors for each category.

2. What does it mean to be set in a particular place by God? What is the purpose for setting you?

3. What is a budding prophet, and what are some of the characteristics?

4. Discuss the importance of a budding prophet's understanding the need to be able to "go forth and stand."

CHAPTER 12—Who Qualifies for the Prophetic?

Not everyone qualifies for the prophetic office, prophetic ministry, prophetic gifting, or basic prophetic. There has to become "a making" before one is actually qualified to be used in these areas of ministry. Those who are senior prophets must understand the importance of qualifying for this office or area of the prophetic. In studying biblical prophets, we come to understand that there was a period of "making" before "using."

The Beginning Stages

The "making" is necessary in order to ensure accuracy. Let's look at the beginning stages of some of the Old Testament prophets.

The prophet Isaiah:

> **In the year that King Uzziah died I saw also the Lord sitting upon a throne, high and lifted up, and his train filled the temple. Isaiah 6:1**

The fact that Isaiah said, "*In the year that King Uzziah died I saw also the Lord,*" puts a question in my heart. The question I have is, "What relationship did Isaiah have to King Uzziah, causing him not to see the Lord before?" Isaiah kept close watch on King Uzziah. Isaiah watched him closely enough that it was only after King Uzziah died that he was able to see the Lord. Many times we will find that we will have to separate from the people and things that have so captivated our attention. This is the sure way that the Lord can speak to us accurately, and that we hear Him without interference (2 Chron. 26:22).

In Isaiah 6, Isaiah was able to say, "When King Uzziah died, I saw also the Lord high and lifted up." So, let's conclude with Isaiah, that one of the qualifications to ensure accuracy is to deal with your distractions.

Fine-Tuning the Prophet

When the call of the prophet is on your life, there will be little sparks of prophetic happenings, just enough prophetic sparks to make you interested. In this season come challenges to prove whether you are hearing the voice of God or other voices. One voice calls you closer to leadership, one voice calls you away from leadership, and still another calls you toward opportunity. Now, the big question is, "Which is correct?"

Did God Call You?

The calling may be one of opportunity, but because of immaturity at this point in the prophetic, it is not yet time to go forth. The voice that is calling you away from present leadership may cause you to leave incorrectly by not being properly released into the prophetic.

When this happens, you are unsure of the voice you hear. "Which voice is correct?" At the same time, you are unsure of what to do. You are being developed! Where do you go when you are hearing all of these voices and have no direction? This is where senior prophets or sometimes prophetic pastors come into play. They may have gone through prophetic seasons and have an understanding of the prophetic. The Word says that **God** places us under governors and tutors until we have matured (Gal. 4:1-3).

Many times we refuse to be governed or tutored because we believe we hear God well enough. Yet, there is a new level of hearing in accuracy that God desires to bring us to.

Key point: *I have noticed that many people who have a call in the area of the prophetic have a tough time receiving correction.*

There is a need to be able to receive the correction to a word given, or given in your spirit. The senior prophet will judge your prophecy. You must be able to receive it without thinking that someone is coming up against your ability to hear God. Proper interpretation of a word given by God, or to a vessel receiving, is often missed by the recipient.

Key point: *This is the testing period that will prove how well you matured in the area of being submissive and receptive to the man or woman of God who is over you.*

118

The proving season is a very important period in the life and ministry of the prophet. Some may think that surely it should not take that long. God gave me a word. He called me to the office of the prophet. It took me ten years to get there. There had to be some additional things burned out of my life so that my hearing would not be affected or infected. This process was necessary for my family, for the body of Christ, and for me. My hearing had to be correct.

Can You Handle Being Disliked?

This is a very popular test of prophetic people. Everyone wants to be liked. Yet, you will find prophetic people who will go overboard to try to get someone to like and appreciate them. Anyone who will stand in the prophetic role must come to know that he or she will be one of the most disliked people among the unsaved and Christian world.

Can You Take Loneliness?

Seeing that you will be one of the most disliked people, loneliness is almost inevitable. If you cannot stand loneliness, which is one of the tests, you certainly are not ready to be a prophet, nor a prophetic person. The prophet is one who often stands alone. Once you have gone through what I call the "prophetic process," you will have many periods in your life when you actually want to be alone. Being alone in many cases is the only way that you can hear God accurately.

I trained myself to hear God under any circumstance by studying in crowds. Take the challenge to hear God while there is noise around you. Your word level gets tested in this season of your life. You can never be fine-tuned without the Word of God and prophetically trained individual in your life. Many people may prophesy, but that is not an indication that they are prophets or prophetically trained.

The Test of Being Offended

Offense hinders your ability to hear accurately. Jesus said that offense must come. Offenses will hinder your ability to hear. Until we can get past offense, we are not ready to occupy the office of the prophet. The real test of whether we have been

NOTES

119

freed from offense is the public rebuke from leadership, rightfully or wrongfully. The test is whether we can take that rebuke and still serve well—not offended.

Handling Intimidation

One of the greatest tests in my life that I had to deal with (in its season) was the test of handling intimidation and not slipping off into a spirit called "jealousy" or "competition." When God started the process of molding me as a prophet, I fought with the spirit of intimidation. If you are going to be the prophet whom God has called you to be, you have to be able to handle intimidation without welcoming any of its companion spirits, lest you be hindered from entering your season in the prophetic. There will be periods when you will feel the need to compete with someone who seems to intimidate you. It could be the one you are submitted to. It could be someone you admire. Regardless of who it is that intimidates you, you must understand that if you can be intimidated, then you are not ready to be released as a prophet. The prophetic is not an area of competition.

When someone intimidates you, it means that the influence that comes from, or seemingly comes from, someone prevents you from walking in the door of who God says that you are. Often times there will be spirits of intimidation that will rise up when you begin to prophesy. If you can be intimidated, that very spirit of intimidation will show up at the time when God wants to use you prophetically.

So before you can be used of God in the area of the prophetic, allow every ounce of insecurity to burn out because that is where intimidation stems from. Intimidation about or regarding an individual is never because of someone else. It is because of your uncertainty and insecurity.

Can You Take Rejection?

Can you take rejection from your leader or those close to you without feeling physically, mentally, emotionally, or spiritually *crushed*? If you cannot take being rejected, then you are not ready for prophetic ministry. Can you really give a prophetic word and not be or feel rejected if it is not being received? Many times the budding prophet gives a word that he believes he heard from the Lord, and it is not received. How will the budding prophet (you) handle the rejection of God's Word? God wants to see that you can handle rejection and not run, faint, or fizz out.

Remember: *Moses' word was rejected several times, yet God kept sending him back to the same person. (Ex. 5,6,7)*

Jonah was tired of preaching to people who kept falling back into the same sin. He knew God would continue forgiving them (Jonah 1:1-3). Jonah is frequently referred to as a prophet who ran away from God. The analogy of the prodigal son leaving home is referred to in the same respect. Yet, it was not the fact that Jonah ran, but it was the reason for his running that is important. He ran from God because he did not want to see another time that he would preach and prophesy to a people who would repent and change the mind of God. Jonah knew that God was going to forgive Nineveh although he prophesied judgment.

Warning: *Maturity in the prophet will not desire to see chaos, havoc, or damnation to come upon people for any reason. It does not matter what they have done to us or anyone else.*

As a prophet, you do not want to run from God, but commune with Him as friend-to-friend. Your actions will assist you in examining yourself to determine the type of prophet you are becoming.

What Type of Prophet Am I?

The office of the prophet versus the gift—How do I know if I have the office or the gift?

As we come to understand whether we are called or whether it is a gift, we also want to determine if it is a ministry or an office. Below you will find a list of the characteristics that I use to locate the gifts and the calling of God that reside in the house where I am the set man. Out of this, I believe that you will find it helpful to distinguish between the various levels of the prophetic.

Key Point: *It is very important to be sure that everyone functions in the area to which they have been called, ordained, or gifted.*

NOTES

To allow someone to function outside of where he or she has been called, ordained, or gifted will caused utter frustration.

Example: *If one has been called to the office of the prophet and is only allowed to use his gifts, then when he has been released to the office, he will be totally frustrated. If one is only gifted and attempts to stand in the office, he will burn out quickly. The gift works as the Holy Spirit wills. One who stands in the office has his office always. He wears his anointing like a coat.*

Prophetic Calling

1. Basic Prophetic: This is when any believer, through the gifts of the Spirit, speaks to someone or a group for the purpose of edification, exhortation, and comfort. (1 Cor. 14:4) This does not include correction or new direction. It may include a predictive word of prophecy.

2. Prophetic Gifting: These are the people who have impressions, dreams, vision, or other types of revelations. They lack the understanding of what they saw or what was prophetically impressed upon them. This group receives more prophetically than the first group, but they are neither in the office of the prophet nor in prophetic ministry.

3. Prophetic Ministry: Believers whose gifting has been recognized, nurtured, and commissioned in regular ministry and the local church are in prophetic ministry. There is still much symbolism that represents other things that God is saying. Through prophetic teamwork, it is possible to discern much of the interpretation and application of the prophetic revelation.

4. Prophetic Office: This one represents the group that is actually called to the office of the prophet. This is somewhat like the prophetic office of the Old Testament. They often minister in signs and wonders and are known to speak 100 percent accurate words of prophecy. This certainly does not mean that they do not miss. It means that what they speak happens most of the time. Their credibility has been established by a proven track record of accurate prophecies. Do the previous attacks stop? After coming into the office, those previous attacks underline continue. The prophet must master functioning accurately in the midst of being attacked. Eventually you become immune to the people talking, their not believing you, and your being rejected.

Serving Until Your Dreams Die

This is a part of the process. Matthew 10:39 says, *"He that findeth his life shall lose it: and he that loseth his life for my sake shall find it."* Whatever I try to save will be lost. The word says: *"Except the Lord build the house, they labour in vain that build it"* (Ps. 127:1). Joseph had to let his dream die in order for God to breathe life into it. Elisha had to go through the death process before his dream of receiving a double portion could live.

Whenever God gives you a vision of what He wants you to have, He always starts you out with a seed. The seed must always go through a process before it goes through the development of the vision.

You begin with a seed only. When we neglect to be a seed, we neglect to have the harvest or the dream. There is always a waiting period to your calling.

Example: *God spoke to me ten years before I was released as a prophet.*

Key point: *There must be the sanctioning of your call by the one you are tied to.*

The Attitude of the Prophet

You must maintain an attitude of love, appreciation, and worship.

Remember: *You become the voice of God. Therefore, what you say MUST, WILL, and SHALL come to pass.*

1. Love—Love is an essential ingredient in the prophetic. If your anger flares up and love is absent, you can speak someone's destruction.

Understand: *God (creator and destroyer) sat down in order that Jesus (redeemer and salvation) might stand up. What did Jesus say to the disciples when they wanted to call down fire from*

NOTES

heaven (Luke 9:54)? Jesus did not tell them that they were unable to accomplish that task, but he warned them of their spirit of operation, thus displaying and forbidding them in their decision. He gave them vision for the people, letting them know that he came to save, not to destroy.

But he turned, and rebuked them, and said, Ye know not what manner of spirit ye are of. Luke 9:55

2. Appreciate—Raise the value of the recipient of the prophecy. We must know the value of a thing, or a person, regardless of what it looks like. God carried Ezekiel through this test. God asked Ezekiel, " Can these bones live?" Ezekiel looked at the condition and became speechless. Then God said: "… these bones are the whole house of Israel." That is when it became Ezekiel's responsibility to raise the value of them and to speak the Word.

Again he said unto me, Prophesy unto these bones, and say unto them, O ye dry bones, hear the word of the Lord. Ezekiel 37:4

Next God told Ezekiel to prophesy unto the winds.

Then said he unto me, Prophesy unto the wind, prophesy, son of man, and say to the wind, Thus saith the Lord God; Come from the four winds, O breath, and breathe upon these slain, that they may live. Ezekiel 37:9

They would have never become what they were purposed to be until the prophet Ezekiel raised their value by speaking into them.

3. Worship—The prophet is one of those who become a drink offering that is poured out on the altar of service. God says through the apostle and prophet Paul:

Yea, and if I be offered upon the sacrifice and service of your faith, I joy, and rejoice with you all. Philippians 2:17

It is verbal worship that is often the vehicle that really keeps you sane. When the prophet loses his place of worship, he or she may become vulnerable to falling back into sin, depression, bitterness, or unbelief.

Examples: *Elijah running from Jezebel (1 Kings 19:1-4); Jonah under the tree (Jonah 4:6); David hung up his harp after saying, "I will bless the Lord at all times. His praise shall continually be in my mouth." (Ps. 137:1-4); When it seemed as if God had deceived him, Jeremiah said, "I will no more speak in Your name." (Jer. 20:7-9)*

What do prophets do when situations and circumstances happen to cause them to lose their place of worship? The prophet is to stand with that last Word of direction heard from God. There may not be another Word until after the test.

Example: *Sometimes when I think back on my prophetic maturity, all I had was the last Word of direction from God. Through sickness, pain, and utter discouragement, all I had was a Word. As a prophet stepping into the office, that was enough.*

NOTES

CHAPTER 12—Chapter Review

1. There is a making that is required to become qualified as a prophet. What is the primary purpose of the making?

2. Describe some of the processes discussed in this chapter that one goes through to ensure accuracy.

3. Describe the characteristic found at each level of prophetic calling.

4. Discuss the various attitude components that a prophet must maintain.

ABOUT THE AUTHOR

Bishop Rodney S. Walker I is a native of Washington, D.C. and a graduate of Jericho Christian Training College and Spirit of Truth Institute where he received his Doctor of Divinity degree.

Bishop Walker's Spiritual Father is Bishop/Apostle Ralph L. Dennis of Kingdom Worship Center in Baltimore, Maryland. In July of 1998, Kingdom Fellowship Covenant Ministries bestowed upon Bishop Walker the Apostolic appointment to the work of Chief Elder/Overseer. As such, Bishop Walker has previously provided assigned regional oversight in the ministry of the Prophetic ascension gift.

In addition to his many assignments, he is the founder and Senior Pastor of Heritage Church International, which was established in April 1990 and is currently located at 2760 Crain Highway, Waldorf, MD. He also serves as the General Overseer of Another Touch of Glory Ministries.

Bishop Walker founded Another Touch of Glory School of the Prophets in 1999. The school has now gone into much of the United States. Presently, Another Touch of Glory Ministries has schools operating in Baltimore and Waldorf, MD, Raleigh and Wilson, NC, Crestview FL, Land Over MD and Abuja, Nigeria. Bishop Walker has also raised a body of Prophetic Presbyters who assist him in managing the great assignment God has set to his hands.

Bishop Walker is the author and publisher of The Prophetic Prayer Devotional, Raising Prophets of Character, The Prophet's Heart Magazine, Yielding My Best For His Glory Devotional, The Renaissance Prophet's Manual, The Father/Son Encounter, Becoming a Proven Prophetic Voice, and the 21st Century Prophet all of which prove to be phenomenal resources of the serious believer's library.

Ephesians 4 is foundational to his charge and calling, however, one of his dearest accomplishments is that of being a devoted husband to his lovely wife, Pastor Betty Walker, and a loving father to his eleven wonderful children.

Bishop Rodney Walker's ultimate goal is to fulfill all that God has purposed for his life and for those placed in his prophetic and pastoral care. His love for God is evident through his preaching, teaching and zeal in ministry. You will experience the wind of the Spirit through this man of God.

Prophet Walker's ultimate goal is to fulfill all that God has purposed for his life and for those placed in his prophetic and pastoral care. His love for God is evident through his preaching, teaching, and zeal in ministry. You will experience God through this man of God...†

CONTACT INFORMATION

To contact Bishop R. S. Walker please write to:

Bishop R. S. Walker Ministries
2760 Crain Highway
Waldorf, Maryland 20601
Phone: (301) 843-9267
Email: admin@bishoprswalker.com

For more information about Bishop R.S. Walker Ministries, please contact us at:

Bishop R. S. Walker Ministries
2760 Crain Highway
Waldorf, Maryland 20601
www.bishoprswalker.com

other works by the author

The Art of Tongues
Raising Prophets of Character
The Prophetic Prayer Devotional
The Renaissance Prophet's Manual – Teacher Edition
The Renaissance Prophet's Manual –Student Edition Level I
The Renaissance Prophet's Manual – Student Edition Level II
Creating Habits for a Functional Life
21st Century Prophet
Becoming A Proven Prophetic Voice
Foundations of Prophetic Maturity – Coming
Yielding To God's Clarion Call
Tapping Into the Prophet's Anointing – Coming
The Joseph Principle – Coming
The Pre-Existent God – Coming
The Ministry of the Holy Spirit – Coming

To order additional books, CD's, DVD's and downloads please contact:

www.bishoprswalkerproducts.com, www.bishoprswalker.com

or

Kingdom Christian Bookstore
2760 Crain Highway
Waldorf, MD 20601
Voice: (301) 843-9267, Fax: (240) 573-3418